GRACE HAPPENS

ADVENTURES IN EVERYDAY LIVING

TOM ALLEN

For Cathy,
the first reader of everything I write
and the first face I get to see every morning.
Thanks for the journey.

No one is a stranger.
We're all sons and daughters.

— Matt Maher

You are on the road to a future God has
prepared, and along the way there is more
delicious mystery to be encountered.

— M. Craig Barnes

Grace Happens: Adventures in Everyday Living

©2016 by Tom Allen

CP

Published by Clovercroft Publishing, Franklin, Tennessee

Published in association with
Larry Carpenter of Christian Book Services, LLC

www.christianbookservices.com

Cover design and photo editing by
Brandon O'Neill (bfoneill.com)

Photos by Tom Allen

Copy editing by Jim Travisano

Interior graphic design by Tammie Carroll,
N-Visioned Graphics, LLC (nvisioned@mindspring.com)

Printed in the United States of America

A Word Before

Grace means a lot of different things to a lot of different people. Many Christians will tell you grace has to do with the love and kindness that comes our way from God, despite none of us having done anything to either cause or merit it.

I believe that's true.

"I do not at all understand the mystery of grace," says writer Anne Lamott, "only that it meets us where we are but does not leave us where it found us," adding that grace sometimes is also "a ribbon of mountain air that gets in through the cracks."

I think that's true, too.

So is this, from author and psychiatrist Gerald May: "Grace is love happening, love in action. I have seen so much grace in the midst of so much brokenness in myself and others."

Grace doesn't have to be all that high and mighty, either. Sometimes, it's just a word—a word of comfort, of affection, of encouragement. It can be a cool drink on a warm day. A note, an email. A phone call, a text. A song lyric, or a sentence you come across when reading. Grace can show up anywhere, anytime.

Grace, for me, is also unavoidably about laughter. There may be no happier gift than those "laugh until you're crying" episodes. I love these words, from Julian of Norwich, who must have been great fun to hang out with: "The greatest honor we can give to God is to live gladly because of the knowledge of his love."

The prayer Jesus taught us to pray includes these words, directed to His father: "Your kingdom come, your will be done." I think every act of grace, no matter how small, gives the kingdom another foothold here.

What follows are somewhat adapted versions of essays originally published in the *Richmond Times-Dispatch* during the last five years, almost all of them in the paper's Faith & Values column. Mostly, they're about keeping my ears and eyes open for glimpses of grace as I live these days I've been given..

Somewhere in here, I hope, you'll catch a whiff of mountain air—and maybe a few grins, too.

Tom Allen
Richmond, Virginia
August 2016

CONTENTS

Paved With (Mostly) Good Intentions...

I once heard a speaker say that the way we behave when we're behind the wheel can be a good indicator of where we are in our relationship with God. That was worrisome, but I think he was right—driving can often be about how we treat other people, how willing we are to make accommodations for them, how routinely we're able to extend grace.

Having said that, I can tell you that there are many days when God and I aren't on the same highway.

On my morning commute, I take a four-lane road that includes an intersection with a traffic light. Immediately after the light, there's an entrance ramp onto the interstate. Almost every morning, there is tremendous jockeying for position between those who patiently drive in the right lane so they can get on the highway and those who race up the left lane and attempt to insert themselves into the right lane, millimeters before the ramp. It's remarkable how small a space between cars in the right lane one of the left-laners can jam himself into, sometimes earning himself a rather un-Christian salute from a frustrated, brake-hitting right-laner.

Now, as I watch a left-laner speedily approaching

from behind with his turn signal frantically blinking, eyeing the inappropriately small piece of pavement just in front of me, it's become a "how would Jesus drive?" sort of dilemma for me. I've seen drivers speed up to make life as difficult as possible for the left-laners. Is it un-Christian of me to smirk? Maybe. Because I try to live my life as a follower of Jesus, should I just hit the brakes, smile happily and wave Mr. In-a-Hurry over? I don't know. But I have noticed that my response in those kind of situations is usually linked to how I started the day just an hour or so earlier—did I check in with God in some fashion and set a course for the day that included making room for my brothers and sisters, or did I stumble out of the house, immediately begin pushing the buttons on the car radio, and just jump into traffic?

Then there are those annoying speed limits. I've racked up three speeding tickets so far, which probably doesn't make Ernie, my car insurance guy, very happy (not to mention my wife), but what does it mean for my quest to drive in a way consistent with who I'm trying to be? Is it un-Christian to be cited for doing 57 mph in a 45 mph zone? Does it mean I'm suffering from the same kind of "hurry sickness" that seems to afflict the left-laners?

This one, I'll admit, remains a struggle. A men's group I'm part of once decided that we would make a conscious effort, for one week, to observe speed limits because the Bible says to obey civil authorities when they're not in conflict with God's law. Here are a couple of the emails that went around the group later the same day we gave ourselves that assignment:

- "After extensive research, I have discovered that speed limits in and around Richmond are set 10-15 mph below where God wants them."
- "Can't we just give up breathing or something?"

Thing is, I believe that God isn't just interested in the specifically "spiritual" parts of my life—I think He's concerned about how I live all of life, every day. Not because He's watching and waiting for me to make mistakes, but because if I'm going to live my beliefs authentically, it's going to have an impact on all the areas of my life. And I spend a chunk of time each day in traffic, where all kinds of things can happen.

So, while I'm just a guy trying to get from one place to another, I'm also a guy who's attempting to stand for something—even when I'm sitting behind the wheel. If you cut me off…well, just know that I'm trying.

Late in the Fourth Quarter, and I'm Way Behind

When I was eight years old, I knew exactly when and where I would die.

If all went according to plan, I would meet my demise near the back of our church, St. Joseph's, just outside of Nashville, Tennessee, struck down in some tragic event the moment I stepped out of the confessional.

This really wasn't my first choice; it was more a matter of necessity. Coming out of confession would be the only time I could ever die with my third-grade soul pure and clean enough to make my way to heaven. The tragic event had to be quick (and hopefully painless) because within minutes of my confession, I would have inevitably screwed up in any number of ways, somehow besmirching my soul and ruining my eternal prospects.

I'd been told, more than once, that you had to be perfect to get into heaven. So if I died stepping out of the confessional, God would not only be contractually obligated, but honored, to welcome me as I strolled triumphantly through the allegedly-pearly gates. He would be somewhat pleased, but also a bit disappointed because He didn't get the chance to do what He really wanted, which was to smite me for my sins.

He was like that.

It took me a couple decades before I could shed this image of God as the Great (But Somewhat Ticked) Scorekeeper in the Sky, and it's an ongoing project. At times, He still reappears and I have no trouble envisioning Him grimly adding to the list He meticulously keeps of my personal misdeeds.

However, Scorekeeper God, who so dominated my thinking for so long, is a long way from the God that the Old Testament book of Isaiah describes as "wonderful counselor," "prince of peace" and "everlasting father." Scorekeeper God is also a long way from the God that Jesus demonstrated in His encounters with people like us during His sojourn on Earth.

These days, I've come to see God very differently and, I think, more accurately. I attribute some of that to no longer being a third-grader and some to the outlook changes that came with fatherhood. The father-child relationship is an important one in Scripture, and is used regularly to describe how interactions between the Creator and the created are meant to be. It's been very helpful to me to see God from that perspective and to think about the way I try to be a father.

I do not sit around with a pencil, watching my kids and recording their mistakes, hoping for a chance to smite them.

I do not expect them to be perfect, let alone demand that they be.

I do not expect them to jump through some pre-determined hoops in order to make me happy.

I do not burden them with rules about matters such as what they should wear, where they should go, what tattoos they should or should not have, or how they should wear their hair.

Why would God?

Instead, what I want with my now-grown kids is to encourage them, to help them—maybe even, sometimes, to inspire them. I want them to grow strong and whole in all the ways that they can, even more than I want that for myself.

I have come to believe that this is somehow similar to the way God feels about us, His children. Yes, in that description I can feel the tension between a God who loves unconditionally and a God who is willing to overlook just about everything His children do. I will be resolving that tension, between something like grace and something like accountability, for the rest of my life. That's OK.

What's not OK, for me, is to pull out Scorekeeper God and revert to estimating how I'm doing in the most recent edition of the divine scorebook. That's not helpful.

It's also not always easy. However, despite the fact that I haven't been inside an actual confessional in some 30 years, I feel less at risk now.

Hey! Check Out Her Teeth

Out of the corner of my eye at the gym, I saw a boy in his early teens walk by, heading for one of the exercise machines. He looked to be about 14. A few minutes later he walked by again and I realized I was way off. He had to be close to 40, at least. He was just a very small man—not someone with dwarfism, but very short and very slight. I wondered about the reactions he must sometimes get from people.

The hostess at the restaurant where a friend and I were having breakfast showed us to a booth. She smiled, revealing a couple prominent gaps where a couple front teeth had once been. I wondered about the reactions she must sometimes get from people.

My sister, who teaches third-graders in another state, had a woman student-teacher working with her one year who my sister thinks must have weighed well over 300 pounds. I wondered about the reactions she must sometimes get from people.

When I was kid, there was a man who drove by our bus stop each morning on his way to work. He had a facial deformity and all of us at the bus stop would wait for him to go by so we could gawk and laugh. Unfortunately, I don't have to wonder about the reactions he must sometimes get from people.

We make an amazing amount of snap judgments about people every day based entirely on the way they look. It's a habit almost all of us acquired as we grew up—clearly, our culture worships at the altar of appearance.

The God I try to worship thinks differently—in fact, in a completely opposite way (as so often seems the case when comparing our thoughts with God's). "The Lord does not look at the things man looks at. Man looks at the outward appearance, but the Lord looks at the heart," says the

Old Testament book of Samuel.

What an incredible injustice we do to someone when we make assumptions about them based on their looks, taking no account of their heart, their spirit, the way they think—the things that really make them who they are.

Once I found myself standing in the hospital room of a friend who had, sadly, died not long before I arrived. She was still in the bed, and looking at her, it was immediately and painfully clear that the characteristics that were uniquely hers were gone. Her heart, her spirit, the way she thought—everything that animated her and made her who she was—were no longer in the room. And while she looked much the same as she always had, she also looked unmistakably different.

Who we are, really, is a tangle of intangibles. What others see are our tangible bodies, which are far quicker and easier to form an opinion about than the spirit within. But it's our spirits that feel the pain of some of those opinions, and that's a pain that can be very slow in healing.

What I can so easily lose sight of as I encounter people every day is something a radio DJ reminded me of during a recent morning commute: "Every person you meet loves something, is afraid of something, and has lost something."

Or, as Plato is most often credited with saying, "Be kind; everyone you meet is fighting a great battle."

And in that battle, everyone has been wounded.

I am acquainted with a young man who is wheelchair-bound because of cerebral palsy. He communicates through a keyboard on the chair, which is attached to a computer that "speaks" the words he types. I said hello to him one day as he wheeled by, and he stopped and painstakingly typed for a few moments. A very digitized voice came out of the computer, asking, "Do you like me?"

It was heartbreaking. Behind his question, I felt the words he hadn't typed: "Please look past what you see." Isn't that the same plea made by the small man at the gym, the restaurant hostess—and everyone else?

Oh, Mercy!

One year when I was in college, I spent the summer working on campus in Virginia while the girl I was dating took a job in New Jersey. I didn't have a car or much spare change at the time, which made visiting a bit of a challenge. One weekend, though, I managed to catch a ride to my parents' house, also in Jersey but still a good hour or more from where she was. Both of my family's cars were needed the next day, so a neighbor lent me his wheels to make the rest of the trip.

That night, this young lady and I found ourselves in that car, second vehicle back at a red light. It seemed an opportune moment to engage in a brief lip-lock, so we did. Unfortunately, while doing so, I took my foot off the brake and the car rolled forward, clunking into the rear of car number one at the light.

We had no idea what do to. As we tried to figure it out, a rather large and somewhat scary fellow emerged from the car, took a brief look at his back bumper, and headed our way. Timidly, I rolled down the driver's side window, fervently hoping he wouldn't see that as an opportunity to insert his fist.

He leaned down, growled, "Keep your eyes on the road and off her"—and then returned to his car.

Mercy is a beautiful thing.

Indeed. Ask Florida pastor and author Tullian Tchividjian—or his teenage son. In Tchividjian's book, *One Way Love*, he tells the story of how he and his wife once punished the young man by taking away his car keys and already-dying cell phone. Not long after the grounding began and his son began making everyone's life difficult by "haunting the house like a drug addict in detox," Tchividjian left on a trip, making but one request of the young man: Don't disrespect your mother while I'm gone.

While away, Tchividjian got a phone call from his wife, letting him know that his son was not exactly following directions. He agonized about how to react when he got home, and felt God urging him to show mercy.

After his arrival, Tchividjian called the son aside and told the doom-anticipating youngster he knew about the misbehavior and was most unhappy about it. But he then threw the boy a curve, telling him to hop in the car—they were heading for the phone store to replace his phone.

His son responded by bursting into tears and saying, "I don't deserve a phone."

"It was a happy day," writes Tchividjian, who hastens to point out that it's important for children to experience the consequences of their actions. It's just that here, mercy seemed to be needed even more.

At some level, I think, most of us understand our need to be forgiven. We know something isn't right about the way we live our lives. I know I do, say and think things every day that I'd be a better person for having not done, said or thought. We all have things we'd love to be able to take back.

Jesus called this sin.

Maybe this understanding of our need for mercy is why one of the most oft-repeated sections of the Biblical book of Isaiah, which is known for both being very unsettling and very comforting, is this: "Come now, let us reason together," says the Lord. "Though your sins are like scarlet, they shall be white as snow; though they are red as crimson, they shall be like wool."

Later, in Ephesians, God is described as being "rich in mercy." Writer Brennan Manning describes him as being "infinitely compassionate with my brokenness." And because that is true, none of us has to feel like, on our own, we must stand before him "white as snow." Who among us could? We're not perfect and won't ever be.

Thank God He doesn't expect us to be. Mercy is, indeed, a beautiful thing.

Free Ride

Mrs. Newman, my ninth-grade English teacher, had given me detention.

She was petite, strict and, from my freshman-in-high-school perspective, definitely getting on in years. She was also someone with whom it was best not to tangle. I don't remember exactly why she "asked" me to stay after school, but I'm sure I deserved it. I'm also certain we had a bit of a chat and I was given some work to do while I was there, but I don't remember those details, either.

What I do remember is that having detention caused me to miss my bus and that home was probably three or four miles away. I decided to head out to the main road and begin hitchhiking. I stood for a while watching cars blow by me, and was getting a bit discouraged about my ride prospects when a little green Chevy Vega (yes, Vega) went by, slowed and pulled over. Delighted, I ran over and hopped in.

Behind the wheel was Mrs. Newman.

After I overcame the initial shock and my desire to sprint away, we had a perfectly jolly ride. We chatted, saying nothing about my detention, and she dropped me off in my driveway. After that, I became one of Mrs. Newman's biggest fans. I no longer thought of her as quite so old and strict—she was an actual human being. Who knew? I made sure I had at least one class with her every year for the rest of high school.

When I think about that incident these days, I'm torn between two feelings, one happy and one a little bit sad.

The happy part is the incredible influence a teacher can have on a kid. One day senior year, I walked into Mrs. Newman's class just as it was getting ready to start and she was preparing to hand back some essays she'd graded. As I passed by her desk, she looked up and said, "You're a pretty good writer, Mr. Allen."

I'm not sure most adults understand the impact an unsolicited compliment can have on a young person. I am pretty sure, though, that most teachers do. They make that kind of impact on students all the time. Not only did what Mrs. Newman said make my day, it helped solidify my plans to pursue a career in some kind of journalism or writing. With one seemingly-casual remark, she bolstered my confidence in a meaningful and lasting way. It makes me very happy to know that there are people like her doing that in schools everywhere, every day.

Years later, when I had my first column published, one of the best things about the day was being able to cut it out and mail it to her. She wrote back, too, in her impeccable penmanship.

The thing that makes me sad about Mrs. Newman and her little green Vega is that I'm not sure she would have felt comfortable pulling over and picking me up if the situation had happened today. We now live in a very different, some-what scary and highly-litigious world.

Today, teachers are almost universally advised, by both their school systems and professional associations, to be very, very careful in student interactions and not to be alone with a student under almost any circumstances. And having a student in your car, certainly if you're off school property, can be a recipe for serious problems. It's far too easy for careless and/or false words by a student to torpedo the otherwise-successful career of an educator.

And so I wonder how Mrs. Newman and I might have found a way to connect today. I was extremely im-mature, and she had a lot to do. I doubt I would have managed to reach out to her. I like to think we would have found a way.

I hope so, because I would have missed a really great ride.

You Could Look It Up — Or Just Look Up

If you can contort yourself enough to climb out the lower half of a window in my oldest daughter's bedroom, you can make your way out onto part of the roof on the back of our house. It can be an outstanding perch. One of the coolest experiences I've ever had as a dad, and as a human being, was out on that roof with that daughter one night, lying on our backs, talking and looking up at the stars.

She's gone on to college and beyond now, and I'm not sure I remember a lot of what we talked about that night—but I'll always remember being out there with her.

There's something about the sky.

Stars, clouds, lightning, streaks of amazing blues, pinks, oranges and purples: Something about the vastness and beauty of the sky, if you look at it for a little while, can stir something vast and beautiful within us (though somewhat smaller, I'm pretty sure).

I think I know why. Psalm 19, said to have been written by King David, puts it like this: "The heavens are telling the glory of God; they are a marvelous display of his craftsmanship. Day and night they keep on telling about God. Without a word...their message reaches out to all the world."

Part of the heavens' message, it seems, has something to do with eternity and timelessness. As clouds roll in, by or over, the sheer immensity of it all seems to encourage me to slow down a bit, suggesting that I can probably find a little different perspective to whatever's on my mind if I'll take a minute and just absorb the panorama above.

There's a constancy to the sky, too. No matter where I am or when I happen to be there, the sky is there, too, both moving and still above me, at once changing and unchanging. People seem to like talking most about sunrises and sunsets, and they are indeed indescribably beautiful. But so is the ordinariness of the sky during the day and at night. Like its Maker, the sky can be a powerful and yet reassuring presence.

It can also be a presence that lifts me like no other. I think my days would grow in peacefulness and trust if I made more time just to look up. I think it could change me.

A fresh-out-of-college couple I know tries to make time on as many of their dates as they can to "chase sunsets." Is there any way you could have a bad date after that?

Life, however, isn't all puffy clouds and sunsets, and neither is the sky. It can look foreboding, frightening and even a bit out of control, reminding us that creation and its Maker are also, in the words of spiritual writer Brennan Manning, "an awesome, incomprehensible and unwieldy Mystery."

Pulitzer Prize-winning author Annie Dillard once traveled to Yakima, Washington to view a total eclipse of the sun that was to happen in the morning, and found the experience overwhelming and even a bit terrifying. "I was out of my depth," she wrote. "In the sky was something that should not be there. In the black sky was a ring of light. It was a thin ring, an old, thin silver wedding band…the heart screeched…the sun was too small, and too cold, and too far away, to keep the world alive."

After a time, the eclipse passed and, Dillard says, "We blinked in the light."

Many of us look to the sky, believing that the light will always return, eventually, for us to blink in once again. A pastor I have great respect for once spoke of the sacredness of creation and said, "Let nature be your rabbi." Rabbi means "teacher," and the sky has much to teach us.

It was good of God to leave us such an ever-ready instructor overhead.

The Family Faces the Heat

On a very toasty New Jersey summer day when I about 13, my mother and grandparents took all six of us kids for a day at the beach in Atlantic City, about an hour's drive from home. (Wisely, Dad went to work.) Wandering the board-walk in the early afternoon, the heat got to my youngest sister, Vicki, who was only a few months old at the time.

Mom pulled our stroller under the shade of the semi-expansive awning of a boardwalk shop, seeking a bit of relief for all of us, especially the now-wailing Vicki. We basked in the momentary coolness, but her somewhat high-decibel crying continued.

Very quickly, the shopkeeper, an older man, marched out his front door and demanded that we move on, as we were "bad for business."

Mom tried to explain what we were doing, but he re-mained unmoved. When we did the same, he disappeared back into the store and returned carrying a long metal rod with a little hook on the end.

Stunned, we all watched him as he used it to roll up his awning. Somehow managing to pull off an expression both triumphant and disdainful, he sauntered back into the store, leaving us back in the heat.

Now, in a world where innocent people are being killed and children are abused every day, rolling up an awning can't really be considered an act of monumental cruelty. But it was definitely not cool.

You know what might have been? I'm thinking maybe a glass of water for a frazzled mother and her little daughter.

I have no idea where that gentleman was in his per-sonal spiritual journey and, since this was a good 40 years ago, I assume he's now continuing it somewhere beyond Planet Earth. But when I think of him, I think of words from the Biblical book of James, thought by most scholars to have been written by one of Jesus' brothers:

"What's the use of saying you have faith if you don't prove it by your actions?...Suppose you see a brother or sister who needs food or clothing and you say, 'Well, good-bye and God bless you; stay warm and eat well—but then you don't give that person any food or clothing. What good does that do?...Faith that doesn't show itself by good deeds is no faith at all."

Our world is in desperate need of some faith lived out, and I don't believe much of that happens through the plans and posturing of our political or military leaders. I think the change we need is much deeper and much more likely to come about through the combined movement of the hearts and minds of individual people—people who allow themselves to be touched by the needs of others and by our common humanity. People who allow God to speak into their hearts.

Almost none of us will have the opportunity to effect large-scale change; all of us have numerous opportunities to reach out and connect with people around us. Individual contact is not just our only option—it's the way forward.

"It is the person that matters. I believe in person-to-person encounters," said Mother Teresa. "Help one person at a time, and always start with the person nearest you."

That little philosophy, lived out, continues to have an impact, long after the diminutive nun has also gone to continue her spiritual journey elsewhere (where I wonder if she's had a chance to chat with Awning Man).

So, here's who I think really holds the key to making our world a better place: Atlantic City shopkeepers. OK, maybe that's a bit too much responsibility for one board-walk, especially since it's located in New Jersey (I can say that—I did most of my growing up there). How about re-tailers around the globe? Taxi drivers. Lawyers. Grocery store cashiers. Bank tellers. Truck drivers. CEOs. Custodians. Me. You.

And, in a special way, owners of awnings.

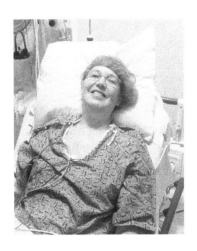

I'll Call Ya...

Few things in life have motivated me to pray like being on a hospital gurney did. True, I was only having cataract surgery, which in today's world is not really a big deal. It does, however, still involve a bit of slicing and dicing of one's eye, so as the gurney rolled toward the operating room, God and I were having a fairly intense conversation. More accurately, God was having to listen to a fairly intense monologue from me.

More recently, and for more serious surgery, my wife got the gurney ride. Once again, I delivered a most sincere speech to my Creator.

Why do so many of us do that? Why is it that we tend to treat God like the "Great 911 Operator in the Sky"?

God: Celestial 911, this is the Almighty. What is your emergency?

Me: My wife is on a gurney.

God: Thanks for letting me know. I'm on it.

Me: Awesome. I appreciate that. Let's chat again next time this happens, OK?

God: *Click.*

It's kind of like this: We have a cat that could not possibly care less about my existence, and generally ignores me completely. However, let me approach the kitchen counter to make a sandwich and let her catch a whiff of ham or tuna, and I am suddenly the coolest guy ever. She races to my side and rubs incessantly against my leg for as long as necessary, looking up at me with undying devotion. The moment I drop a bit of the ham or tuna on the floor, she's done with me again.

I'm pretty sure God thinks differently about us than I do about our cat—I really hope so, anyway, because all I really want to do is boot the cat when she acts like that. Nobody wants to feel used—including, I suspect, God.

I believe what He wants from us is an actual relationship, a desire that we share with Him the life He's given us. Relationships are what we're built for; they're why we get out of bed in the morning. Learning to have and build relationships with one another and with God is, to me, a big part of why we're here.

I actually had reason to call 911 recently, for the first time ever. The dispatcher was very kind and very competent, but very little passed between us. A friend had an important need and she was able to help. I wouldn't know her if she walked past me on the street, and our "relationship" is over.

All this has gotten me to thinking about a guy named Enoch, who has now become one of my favorite guys in the Bible. He's only mentioned a couple times, and little is known about him. But what stands out is the way he's described: He was a man "who walked with God." In a list of men in a section of the book of Genesis, Enoch is the only one described this way. Because his life was marked by this everyday closeness with God, Enoch is later described in the book of Hebrews as "one who pleased God."

I want to live the way Enoch did. "Walking with God" sounds like a much better way to live life than making the occasional frantic phone call to Celestial 911 does. And it doesn't just sound better: I think it's the only way life really works.

One more thing: Because I believe God is able to have a personal relationship with each one of us, I'm open to the idea that some things in life are beyond coincidence. I can't, of course, point to them with absolute certainty. All I can do is describe a recent example: Not long after I'd begun thinking about Enoch and the idea of "walking with God," I was on a train, reading a novel a friend had just recommended to me. Thoroughly enjoying the story, I turned a page and hit a sentence that made me shut the book and stare out my window for the next bunch of miles.

The sentence? "Life was very different when you walked through it."

Life in the Slow Lane

John Ortberg, a nationally-known pastor and author, was moving into a new ministry position several years ago, a job with a long list of responsibilities. Seeking to make the transition smoothly, he called another minister who'd been a mentor to him and asked for some advice.

"What do I need to do to be spiritually healthy?" Ortberg asked.

There was a long pause before the voice on the other end of the line said, "You must ruthlessly eliminate hurry from your life."

Ortberg quickly scribbled that down, pen poised for more. Another long silence. Ortberg pressed for additional items to add to his list.

"There is nothing else," said his mentor. "You must ruthlessly eliminate hurry from your life."

So there it is: my only New Year's resolution for next year. I'm going to be very intentional about applying the brakes and living more of life in the slow lane. I will not hurry anyone or anywhere and, as a result, I will become a picture of spiritual health.

Yeah, count on that.

I can get aggravated in slow-moving lines, and impatient with people who are derailing what I really want to be doing. Aggravated and impatient people are no fun to be around. But it's not just that; "aggravated and impatient" is way out of tune with life as God designed it to be lived.

I've come to believe that there's great wisdom in the simple advice given to Ortberg by his mentor. There's more than I know going on in every moment, and I'll miss almost all of it if I'm living in a state of acceleration. In "Top Gun," Tom Cruise reveled in his "need for speed," and many of us seem to have taken that phrase to heart. Speed is appropriate and probably amazing if you're in a jet fighter; I don't think it works as well after you've landed.

Strange as I once would have thought this to be, one of my favorite hours of last year was spent sitting in an Adirondack chair on a patio at a hotel in the Virginia mountains and watching a chipmunk go about his life in the nearby bushes. Every once in a while he'd get up on his hind legs and check me out too, although I wasn't doing anything nearly as fascinating as he was. We just hung out together for a while.

On the seventh day God rested, and rest is a consistent theme in Scripture. Jesus never seemed too hurried to spend time with the people He met along his way. I think of Him, an island of measured calm in a tempest created by some angry and scheming men who dragged a woman "caught in adultery" before Him and demanded justice, which to them meant immediate stoning. The Bible describes Jesus bending down to write carefully in the sand with His finger, ignoring the clamor, perhaps collecting His thoughts before speaking these words for the ages: "Let him who is without sin cast the first stone."

To help remind me to travel slow and steady through my days, my daughter has gotten me a funky little sculpture of a turtle. He sits (rather still, I have to say) on my computer and casts sideward glances at me during the workday. He's helpful to have around.

This conversation, this meal, this view, this encounter. Whatever it is, it's right now and in some way it's a gift—and a gift that will never be given again. I don't want to miss it. I want to savor those moments, experience them for what they might and can be, without mentally racing ahead to whatever's next. Those moments are all we've really got.

I'm going to attempt to live them with less speed and more deliberation. Ruthlessly.

Brought to You By...

To live in our media-driven culture, and to be anywhere this side of comatose, is to be bombarded every day with a steady stream of messages aimed at our hearts and minds. While a lot of this can just be a kind of background noise, I think we ignore it at our own peril because over time we become, in many ways, what we absorb.

Advertisers, artists, media consultants and, not least of all, others we encounter are all attempting to shape our thoughts and values, all the time. What's getting through? What am I letting get through, and what kind of impact is it having on the person I am and am becoming? On the person God created me to be?

To check this out, I decided to pay more careful attention for a day and see what happened.

Things got going pretty early. On the way to work, among the several billboards that went by was one for a "gentlemen's club," offering "pure pleasure" and featuring a woman who looked very interested in getting to know me. I have no doubt there is some pleasure to be found by dropping by the club, but I suspect there's nothing pure about it.

The billboard on the other side of the highway encouraged me to stop and buy a Powerball ticket so I could pick up a cool $60-something million. In infinitesimal print were my infinitesimal chances.

The "sex and money" drumbeat quickly established itself as a theme for the day. When I got to the office and checked my e-mail, I found an offer to purchase a wonder drug that would correct an anatomical deficiency I apparently suffer from, as well as a chance to "consolidate my debts," which must be why I need the Powerball money.

I clicked on my Facebook page, where Mark Zuckerberg and his colleagues are pretty much watching, through my screen, every move I make. So, ever since I hit a somewhat significant birthday a couple years ago, my page regularly greets me with advertisements about hot "senior" singles to be found in my area, evidently not concerned that my marital status, noted on the page, is "married." (Incidentally, the women in those ads don't look tremendously "senior," but they do look every bit as eager to hang out with me as the woman on the billboard.)

Later, as I flipped through a sports magazine, a hotel chain told me, over a picture of happy folks mingling in the hotel bar, that "The more 'more' you have, the more you have to have more." Or I could drive a particular import and "get used to hot girls whistling at you." Maybe those whistles are why there's an ad further back in the publication headlined "Paternity Questions?"

And I hadn't turned on the TV yet.

I'm not out to bash the producers of all these messages. They're just doing their jobs, giving us what they think we want. And to be fair, I also passed several billboards that had much more positive messages and saw some well-intended, clever advertising in the magazine. But overall, few of the values and attitudes I saw being presented seemed especially helpful.

Why is it that a huge chunk of the messages our culture puts out plant seeds that I don't really want to see grow?

And why do I so often choose those messages? Why am I sometimes so slow, so reluctant to turn to the One whose message has remained unchanged throughout human history? Jesus' message is the one I would like to come through to me most clearly, the one I want to use to filter all the other ones through. It's interesting that one of the most popular translations of the Bible in bookstores today is called The Message.

Jesus once said, "If you hold to my teaching, you are really my disciples. Then you will know the truth, and the truth will set you free." Truth and freedom: Only one message offers that. My days would be far better spent tuned in to that one, and to that One.

What are we tuning in to? What are we turning into?

Gumby Stretches Out

There's an ancient story that tells of a spiritual seeker, who stood near a church one day and pondered the issue of suffering as he watched the crippled, the beaten and the beggars go by. "Great God," he prayed, "How is it that a loving Creator can see such things and do nothing about them?" After a long silence, God replied, "I did do something about them. I made you."

This week, I'm especially grateful that God made Gumby and Jason.

A little back story: Cathy, my wife, is recuperating after some very significant surgery. During her recovery, she's using a walker to help her get around, until the balance and strength issues caused by the operation improve.

Last Sunday morning, we made our joint descent of the stairs, Cathy holding onto me for dear life. Downstairs, she grabbed the walker, cruised into the kitchen and opened the cabinet where she keeps her medications.

Not more than two minutes later, when I joined her in the kitchen, I found her pitched forward over the walker, face planted on a small stack of recycle-ready newspapers on the counter beneath the cabinet. Her eyes were open, but she didn't respond to my voice, no matter how loud I got, or to my gentle shaking.

I've carefully avoided all things medical my entire life, so I had no idea what was going on. I wondered if she was having some kind of seizure. I carefully lifted her head and shoulders, and she was completely limp in my arms, so I lowered her to the floor. She stared toward the ceiling, but still without any indication that she could either hear or see me. If there's been a more frightening instant in my life so far, I can't think of it at the moment.

Enter Gumby and Jason.

By this time, I had begun a serious conversation with

the good people at 911. Of course, part-way through that phone call, Cathy blinked a couple times, looked around, and informed me that there was no reason on earth to involve those people. I disagreed, as politely as I could, and in a few minutes an ambulance bearing Gumby the paramedic and Jason the EMT pulled up in front of the house.

While I'm sure God made them for lots of reasons, one of them was certainly for days like this. Calm and cool, they arrived in our home from a place of kindness and compassion within themselves, an amazing place I've had the opportunity to see a lot of health care professionals living out of lately. Gumby and Jason (apparently, most people in Fire Station World go by a nickname) were able to care for and comfort Cathy and me and still walk us through what had happened, all the while managing to assure us they had the situation covered.

They entered into our chaos and managed to bring along a sense of peace.

They took Cathy's vital signs, asked lots of questions, and listened carefully to our answers. They were thoughtful, concerned and in no hurry to wrap up and move on. In the end, they (and Cathy, who is a nurse) decided all this was very likely the result of an episode of low blood pressure combined with post-surgery pain. We opted against a trip to the emergency room, and we've watched Cathy carefully since, being sure she's getting enough liquids, food and rest.

Jesus said he came "not to be served, but to serve," and I believe we're most in tune with our Creator when we're reaching out to others to help and to serve. Gumby and Jason reached out to us at a time when we surely needed it, just as thousands of first responders everywhere do, all day every day. Some might say they're just doing their job. I say, if you're built for it, what an amazing and fulfilling job it must be to do.

God can often seem like a faraway kind of guy, a distant concept. There's a saying popular in some faith-based circles that one of the things we're supposed to be for one another is "God with skin on." We all have chances to do that, every day.

It's a beautiful thing when it happens. Ask Gumby and Jason.

Slap a Label On It

When I was a kid, I got what was then considered an extremely hip gadget, and I was every bit as excited about it as any kid today when he gets his first smartphone. It was a shiny plastic Dymo labelmaker, and I spent hours feeding different colors of tape into it, spinning the wheel with all the letters on it, and creating labels for a large majority of my earthly possessions.

I put my name on my tennis racket, identified what was in my storage boxes (in case I forgot what I'd put in either of them), and was generally quite impressed with my new-found organizational skills.

Looking back, it may have been my worst toy ever.

I can't really blame Dymo for this, because it's clearly not the company's fault, but this may have been part of the launch of a very troublesome lifetime habit for me and for most everyone I know: organizing and understanding the world by making and applying easy-to-use labels.

My Dymo is probably buried somewhere today, doing an excellent job of being non-biodegradable. These days,

I'm trying my best to get rid of the one in my head, too. I've come to believe that for me the best, and just about only, use for labels is on file folders. I understand how important it can be, in some situations, to "name" something--doing so can be an important first step toward healing. But when it comes to what really counts, people and relationships, for me labels have not been at all helpful.

Labels are just an easy, shorthand way of not having to deal with the complexity of the person in front of us. They allow us to stay in our comfort zones. She's a right-winger. He's a liberal. He's a homophobe. She's a racist. He's just a wacko.

Actually, they're all human, flawed and broken, like me.

One of the things people found (and continue to find) so unsettling about Jesus was his total disregard of labels. He not only ignored them, He thumbed His nose at them— figuratively, although I don't think literally would have been entirely out of character.

For instance, there were few labels in Jesus' Jewish culture more derogatory than "Samaritan." The Jews regarded Samaritans as half-breeds and heretics, and the hatred on both sides ran so deep that the religious leaders of both taught that it was wrong for Jews and Samaritans to even speak to each other. Angry confrontations were not unusual.

So who's the hero in one of the most well-known of Jesus' parables? Not the two religious leaders who also appear in it, but the "Good Samaritan," the only one who reaches out to help a man in need. That would have been flat-out scandalous to label-using listeners.

Jesus also has an important conversation with a Samaritan woman at a well, which was label-bashing in two ways: First, she was Samaritan and second, she was a she. Women at the time were clearly second-class citizens, dependent on men for their support and for their very identity.

Yet women, even one widely thought to have once

been a prostitute, were with Jesus throughout his public life, even to the cross and, significantly, as the first witnesses at the empty tomb.

Tax collectors of the time were regarded as pretty close to the scum of the earth. Collaborating with the occupying forces of Rome, they padded their pockets by overcharging their fellow Jews for the Roman taxes, earning themselves a much-reviled label.

Yet Jesus called one, Matthew, out of his tax-collecting booth to join His band of disciples and very publicly dined at the home of another, Zaccheus.

It's no wonder the label-makers who hung around Jesus were often left foaming at the mouth.

Jesus physically touched lepers, another egregious no-no; trash-talked the most highly-regarded religious leaders in the community when necessary; took the side of social outcasts; praised the faith of a Roman centurion; and generally upset everyone's apple cart. The man was the walking definition of "countercultural."

And, according to the most reliable records we have, He never owned a labelmaker.

The Long Arm of the Law

"Probably my worst call ever happened right there," said Lt. Jim Sizemore, nodding in the direction of a small brick home as we cruised by in his unmarked Hanover County Sheriff's car. On a quiet Friday afternoon, the yard was so overgrown it was tough to tell if anyone still lived in the house.

"It was a double homicide," Sizemore explains, adding that a third person had also been shot but survived. A 24-year law enforcement veteran in Hanover, Sizemore had been the first officer to arrive on the scene. While that wasn't a typical day at the office, "We often see people at their worst," he says.

Sounds like an excellent environment in which to lose one's faith.

Perhaps for some, but not for Sizemore. "If anything, as I've gained some age, some life experience and hopefully some wisdom," he says, "my faith has gotten stronger. I'm more compassionate. Early in my career, I really just wanted to get there and help. Now I find myself praying that God will look after these people and help me help them.

"I used to think I had to do everything on my own," he says, "because people call us to solve their problems. But I can't do it myself. I've put my faith in Christ and let him work with me and with people's issues. It comes down to what you're going to hang your hat on."

Sizemore is in charge of the weekday night shift for the county sheriff's office. The officers he leads gather in the briefing room before the shift begins for instructions that include reports from the day shift, updates from surrounding jurisdictions, and a wide range of information on anything from training opportunities to a lengthy funeral procession that's going to cross a big chunk of the county late in the afternoon. Then 16 men and women in uniform head out for whoever and whatever awaits them on the streets.

"I'm not sure how you could do this work without some kind of faith," says Col. David Hines, Hanover County's Sheriff.

Terry Sullivan wasn't sure for a while if he could do the work with his faith. After 13 years on Hanover's force he felt a strong pull to the pulpit so he left, entered seminary, and eventually began a church in Florida. Three years later, he came back and is now an investigator in charge of the sheriff's office of criminal intelligence as well as serving as a part-time associate pastor at a local Baptist church.

"At the time, that was the only way I thought I could minister full-time," Sullivan says of his departure for seminary, "but I realized I could still work in a secular workplace. Our values and mission here are very close to the same ones we have in the church—to serve and protect. We go out, reach out to people and offer help. I tell people I do more ministry now than I've ever done."

Sullivan also oversees the department's chaplaincy program, in which local clergy volunteer to ride along with officers and are summoned during emergencies, often fielding some very tough questions. "After a very difficult situation, like a fatality, happens," Sullivan says, "we can get, 'Where was God in this?' Those answers aren't in the policy book."

Easy answers are in short supply in the world of law enforcement, and that takes a toll on some officers. "If you've been a police officer for a long time," says Matt Mc-Grain, an investigator, "you can develop a negative attitude about the world, the public and just in general. We see a lot of death and drug abuse.

"Because of my faith, I feel like I've been released from all that," says McGrain, a 21-year Hanover Sheriff's employee. "I try to see the people I deal with, the supposed 'bad guys,' as brothers and sisters who may have taken a wrong turn. Jesus is watching out for them, too. I want to treat them like I'd want to be treated. And, when I do, it creates a much better platform—people are much more likely to open up."

My afternoon and early evening ride-along with Sizemore was my first experience in a police car and, though the car was unmarked, also my first small taste of how officers do their sometimes unpopular work in a fishbowl. One 20-something guy, in particular, eyed us with distaste as we waited at red light, and a motorcyclist who came roaring up behind us on Route 301 suddenly became a model, speed-limit-observing citizen when he got a better look at our car.

"What we do isn't about sitting by the side of the road and writing a traffic ticket," says Sullivan. "It's about helping people succeed in life, and helping provide a safe and secure environment they feel good about raising a family in."

"For a lot of us, it's a calling," says Sizemore.

Doing the Wash

I know the guy who e-mailed this joke to me just meant to share some grins, and thought I'd get a good laugh out of it. He had no idea it would pretty much ruin my morning:

A couple sat at their breakfast table one morning, and the wife watched her neighbor hanging wash outside. "That laundry's not very clean," she said. "She doesn't even know how to wash right. Maybe she's using a lousy brand of detergent."

Every time the neighbor would hang her wash to dry, the wife would make similar comments about what a poor job she was doing.

A couple weeks later, the woman was surprised to see the wash hanging spotlessly on the line and said to her husband, "Look, she finally learned how to do the laundry right. I wonder what happened?"

The husband said, "I got up early this morning and cleaned our windows."

Ouch. I sank a bit in my chair.

Jesus, who loved to teach using parables not very different from that one, had a few thoughts on situations like this. "Do not judge, and you will not be judged. Do not condemn, and you will not be condemned," He said, adding "Why do you look at the speck of sawdust in your brother's eye and pay no attention to the plank in your own eye?"

It's not easy lumbering around with lumber in my eye.

I get irritated with a generally unreliable guy I know who often doesn't return phone calls or follow through on things he says he'll do. Then I remember that I didn't grow up in a family ravaged by alcoholism and don't have to carry around that particular piece of baggage every day.

I know some people who manage to steer just about every conversation we've ever had to some of their own outstanding accomplishments or to the exploits of their unfailingly exceptional and nearly-perfect children. It makes me wish they had a permanent trap door under them, so I could just push a button and be done with it—until I realize that I've got insecurities of my own that probably dwarf theirs. (And that they haven't compared their children to ours.)

I get offended when people make derogatory comments about the way others look, or their politics, or their attitude, or their speech, or whatever. Then I think about some of the remarks I make, and snicker about, when I'm with friends or family.

I find it off-putting when some commentators seem to frame just about every issue as a racial one. Then I remember that I have no idea of what it's actually like to live as a minority in America today.

Someone else I know aggravates me with her persistent attention-seeking and self-centeredness. Then it occurs to me how much of every day I spend acting like I'm the center of the universe.

It's frustrating when some people I know won't venture beyond their comfort zones to try something new I'm sure they'll enjoy. That one is flat-out laughable when I consider my own lifelong battles with anxiety.

Then there are those people who record their every movement on social media for the world to enjoy. OK, these people are still really irritating. Sorry, there are limits.

Yeah, the window I'm looking at life through is pretty well-smudged, and does an excellent job of clouding my view of the laundry hanging on my neighbor's line. What's more, I'm not sure there's enough Windex on the planet to fix that for me. I think it's probably better just to be honest, admit that I've got a window issue, and squint more often. With God's help, hopefully everything will come out in the wash.

Neck and Neck

One of the most heart-rending moments I've experienced as a parent was calling home from the office one afternoon to hear the results of my then-nine-year-old son's student council election. Between sobs, he told me that he'd lost. He was heartbroken and I was helpless to do anything about it.

Later, I watched him, his sisters and their friends do battle in the cutthroat world of college applications and admissions.

Today, I have a friend who gets an e-mail, every single day, telling him where he ranks in his company's nation-wide sales force.

Seems that for about as long as I can remember, a lot of life has been about competition. It's all about coming out on top, being better than someone else. What fun is life without someone to feel superior to?

Every once in a while, I'll read something and a sentence will reach off the page and clobber me. Recently, it was a simple statement written by renowned spiritual writer Henri Nouwen: "We are brothers and sisters, not competitors and rivals." That's not exactly earth-shattering stuff: It's a pretty basic truth of faith. But it's one that has the power to profoundly change my life, if I'll let it.

I understand that competition is a necessary in a lot of

situations, and that it can be downright healthy sometimes. But at our most human level, where we're all pretty much the same, I think it has the power to rob us of our best and highest life.

Competition is usually all about comparison, and going there can be a trip to a dark and dangerous place.

All of us have a strong desire for affirmation and recognition, a need to feel like we're "special." I'd like to blame mine on growing up with five siblings, but the fact is that this desire comes standard in the human equipment package.

And we are special. Jesus says, "The hairs on your head are numbered," and Psalm 139 tells us, "For you created my inmost being; you knit me together in my mother's womb." Throughout Scripture, God assures us that we matter to Him, individually.

It's just that we're not more special than anyone else, and that's where the problem can be. My default mode has been to view others as the competitors that Nouwen talks about. We want to measure ourselves against others—and come out ahead. We want to be more this and more that (including more spiritual) than most people. While that may be a natural desire, I don't think it's a healthy one.

Life with God isn't about competition; it's not something you can win. I don't think it's possible to get more of His attention than others do, or to be more deserving of it. And it shouldn't be.

At times, I've suffered from a world-class case of schadenfreude, a German term for enjoying the misfortunes of others, thinking that maybe the screw-ups of others boosted me in the divine standings. And I don't think I'm alone—Nouwen also says, "That which is most personal is most universal," and I believe he's right.

There's something very liberating about accepting, and trying to live, the fact that we're all brothers and sisters, children of God. It frees me to want, and to work for, what's best for others in my life. It frees me to celebrate their successes, and to love them without jealousy. Most of all, it frees me from the constant strain of having to be ahead of them. I can just be with them, and we can travel together. What a huge relief.

I believe God is very personal, and more aware of what's going on in my mind and heart than I am. That's wonderful to know, but I can't stake any unique claim on Him—He's in the know about every other person on the planet, too. His attention is far broader, deeper and more expansive than I can know. Being a part of His family is a life-changing gift. I shouldn't need to be the favorite son.

I'm doing everything I can to drop out of that competition.

Flipping Fathers Day

I became a father just after 8 o'clock one Sunday morning, almost 30 years ago, not too long after a middle-of-the-night announcement from my wife, Cathy, that her water had broken. Several hours after the emergence of our firstborn, I ventured downstairs to the hospital's cafeteria, in a state pretty close to euphoria, to grab something to eat. As I slid my tray along the railing toward the cashier, she smiled and said, "What did you have?"

"It's a boy!" I blurted, grinning, delighted that some-one had asked, and thinking I must have that "new-father" look all over me.

Her smile morphed quickly into a semi-withering look as she gestured toward my tray. "I meant, 'What did you have to *eat*,'" she said.

This was, of course, not her fault, but she was clearly unaware of how the arrival of Andy, and the later appear-ances of Amy and Emily, had and would forever change the world as I knew it.

The whole pregnancy thing had been somewhat un-real for me—mostly, I think, because I didn't really get it. OK, I had no idea whatsoever what was going on. I wasn't quite as connected to the whole concept, not being the one getting regular elbows in the bladder and other sensitive organs from something inside that was alive and growing.

Sure, Cathy would grab my hand a couple times a day and press it against her belly when there was a lot of movement going on, but what I remember most about that was thinking how queasy it would make me feel to have something moving around inside me. I've always been the only one residing in my body, and I've never been especially eager to add to the number of those on board, so I didn't quite have the reaction she was looking for.

But something happened when Andy popped out, wriggling and wailing (something he does somewhat less of these days, at 27). It was one of those moments when things not only are never going to be the same, but you actually recognize that fact in real time. This was a little human, and one who, while it might still be one of the great practical jokes of all time, we were allegedly responsible for the care and upkeep of.

I knew right then I'd do whatever I could to make his life better.

Well, except for this one thing: When the pediatrician, who was a friend, came in with the consent form allowing him to do a brief procedure on the poor boy called a circumcision, I signed it and began to follow him down the hospital hallway.

"You don't want to be here for this," my doctor-friend told me, sort of grinning but actually quite serious. He talked me into skipping this particular event, though I still felt like I'd let the little guy down a bit already.

When the girls came along, I felt like I had an idea of what to expect in the delivery room. Just to prove that I was still clueless, both Amy and Emily were born face up, which is not the normal way of making one's debut into society. This made the whole process more difficult for Cathy, the shining heroine of these occasions, but was an early indication that the girls would be doing their own thing.

While at times I've thought that maybe my father had the better deal because, back in the day, he got to be in the waiting room hanging with the other dads while his children were born, I'm delighted to have had those moments with each of the kids as they made this whole fatherhood thing official.

So, while most of the Father's Day focus is squarely on Dad, I'd like to deflect it for a minute and say this to Andy, Amy and Emily: From the instants you each appeared on the scene, you've made life for Mom and me so much more meaningful, more precious, more fun, more full, more scary, more difficult, more beautiful, and just way more worthwhile.

We can't imagine it any other way. Happy Father's Day to you, too.

Literally...Really

One night when I was a little kid, I was riding in my back seat perch in the family station wagon when Mom said something about being careful not to look into the bright headlights of oncoming cars. Doing so, she warned from the front passenger seat, could lead to being "blinded."

For several years after that I was scared half to death that I might accidentally glance into the brights of another car and lose my eyesight forever. With visions of white canes and dark glasses in my head, I became the most skilled boy on the planet at averting my eyes on dark roads.

A handful of decades later, I've learned not to take everything so literally.

I thought of this not long ago when a friend said to me, as we devoured some Thai food (and I paraphrase, but only slightly), "You're a semi-smart person. How is it that you can really believe this Christianity stuff?"

I did my best to give her a coherent answer that day, but looking back, I think the best response I have to her question is that there are some things I actually do take literally. I like to think I always will. One of them is this statement made by Jesus: "I am the light of the world. Whoever follows me will never walk in darkness, but will have the light of life."

I've come to believe Jesus to be divine, but not because of any amazing revelation. It's actually more because of some very human behavior: I think I'm a believer largely because of the actions of the men who most closely surrounded Jesus, the very regular guys who spent three years wandering the countryside with him.

For them, life had become pretty good. From very prestigious front-row seats, they were basking in the glow of perhaps the biggest celebrity in their part of the world, seeing crowds and events they'd never anticipated witnessing, and being accorded the kind of stature that can come with being in the famous guy's posse.

But the party ended abruptly in Jerusalem. Now, suddenly, their leader had been very publicly humiliated, tortured and executed—they'd watched the crucifixion happen and lived in fear they were next in line for a similarly-excruciating death. They weren't just laying low: They were cowering behind a barred door, terrified at any moment Roman soldiers would break it down, looking for them with fatal intentions.

That's a fear they had to feel in the pits of their stomachs, their pounding hearts, and just about everywhere else. The light, for them, had been snuffed out.

Yet, somehow days later they were the ones breaking down the door, boldly speaking about Jesus—and almost all of them, indeed, ended up dying martyrs' deaths. To me, that kind of transition, from abject terror to unfettered boldness and courage, could only have happened for one reason: They must have encountered, once again, the man they had last seen crucified. They had to have seen him in a new, risen state.

Because they did, it gets a lot easier to take literally some other things Jesus said, like claiming to be "the way, the truth and the life." Or "the resurrection and the life."

Jesus' little group of followers must have seen a light unlike any they'd ever seen before. And, instead of blinding them, it left them seeing in an entirely different and clearer way than ever before. I'd like to think I catch glimpses with that kind of sight, too. Literally.

There's More to the Story

The 50-something woman stared into the distance out the window of the shuttle van taking the two of us from the hospitality house over to the hospital. "My husband had a double lung transplant two years ago," she said. "He was on his deathbed. He wouldn't have lasted another day without it."

Unsure what to say, I asked how he was doing. "He has pneumonia again," she answered. "He's on a ventilator. We've been in every unit in the hospital and on just about every ventilator."

I liked that she said "we."

Her eyes brimmed with tears when I asked if she knew anything about the person whose lungs her husband now used to breathe. "We found out his name, through the hospital," she said, "and you could send a letter to the family, also through the hospital. We did, but we never heard anything back."

Before getting on the van, I'd had breakfast back at the hospitality house with a couple I guessed were about 70. Their 44-year old son had had part of his lung removed; it was cancerous after 30 years of smoking. "He's still smoking," the father said, with an air of grim resignation.

So many hurting people. And, so often, we have no idea.

I was staying at the hospitality house while my wife had some delicate neurosurgery that we fervently hoped, for the second time, would bring an end to her years of chronic pain.

So many hurting people. I lived in the hospitality house for a week, where the pain can be pretty obvious. I live the rest of my life in places where the pain doesn't show so much.

Four women I know, all who seem to be the kind of

wife any man would be lucky to have, recently made the excruciating decision to end their marriages. Now they're trying their best to navigate the difficult waters of broken relationships, hurting children, the discomfort of friends, and new relationships.

Two men I know, the kind of guys you'd like to have living next door, have recently had to close their businesses because of our struggling economy. They're now jobless and trying to figure out their next move.

Other people dear to me are trying to cope with the loss of parents and other family members, dealing with their own aging, facing the repeated and crushing disappointments of infertility, fighting with close family members, and wondering why they're going to a job they despise every day.

And if you passed them on the street, you'd have no idea. The stories that live behind the faces we encounter every day are a mystery, often known only to a select few, or not to anyone. So many hurting people.

The suffering we do know about, we can't really fix. As much as we'd like to, we usually can't heal the hurting places of our family members and friends, to say nothing of those whose suffering we can't begin to know. I can't fix the man with the double lung transplant and pneumonia, or stop the 44-year-old from picking up his next cigarette, or make my wife's pain go away—though I've tried that last one mightily.

We can, however, have an impact. It is within our power to lighten a burden, if only a little. I think it helps a lot just to know we're not alone. A small gesture of kindness, a word of concern, an e-mail—we have no idea how far that can go. And we must try, because too many of us are walking around in a pile of hurt. In some way, almost all of us are.

In the hospitality house, there was a camaraderie of the hurting. We need that out in the world, too.

Life OFF the Fault-Line

The little drama played out in two acts in the crowded waiting room at the doctor's office.

Act one featured a 40-ish father and his preschooler son, who looked to be about three. The little boy was not inclined to wait patiently with Dad while Mom was in with the doctor, preferring instead to noisily roam the room, re-arrange the magazines, climb on the furniture, and try to get through the door that he knew Mom had gone through earlier.

Throughout, Dad kept up a steady monologue of half-hearted scolding, mostly grinning and addressing his son as "Dude," as in, "Dude, your bottom should be in the chair and your feet on the floor, not the other way around." He also provided narration for the rest of us in the room, sharing his opinion with Dude that his mother's ailment was almost surely psychosomatic.

Act two began when Dad and Dude went off in search of a restroom for a few minutes. A couple who looked about Dad's age began a conversation about what they had just seen, either unaware or unconcerned that they were being heard by most of the room. "Can you believe that kid?" "What is that guy thinking?" "When's the last time you heard a kid say 'yes, sir' or 'no, sir' to an adult?" "And the way they talk, even to their teachers, these days!"

There are a lot of challenging verses in the Bible; that day in the waiting room, this is the one that grabbed me: "If you love those who love you, what credit is that to you? Even 'sinners' love those who love them. And if you do good to those who are good to you, what credit is that to you? Even 'sinners' do that." The speaker is Jesus.

Or, as writer Brennan Manning explains it, "As God rains peace and goodness on the just and unjust alike, so should we. Anyone can love their friends, those with whom we have a mutuality, a reciprocity. True godliness demands much, much more."

I think all of us in the waiting room felt a bit disapproving of Dad's child-rearing tactics and silently agreed with the couple who shared their conversation with us. None of us, however, had offered any help to Dad and Dude or really reacted in any way. It was easier to roll our eyes, literally or figuratively.

Sure, it would have been out of the ordinary to do or say something in an attempt to be helpful, but isn't that what Jesus was saying? Shouldn't there be something a bit "out of the ordinary" about those of us who say we follow Him?

Not long before, I was the first car at a red light at Franklin Street and Shafer Court—right in the middle of the Virginia Commonwealth University campus. It's a great place to be caught at a red light because it has to be one of the top 10 people-watching spots in town. So, as I waited for green, I took in the parade of pedestrians passing just a few feet in front of my hood.

I drove on when the light changed, and thought about what I'd just thought about. A sample from windshield time at Franklin and Shafer: "How can she even walk with heels that high? That's gotta hurt." "A guy his age doesn't look right on a skateboard." "No way I'd let my daughters wear an outfit that revealing."

Why is fault-finding so often our default position? It feels more than a bit ironic, given that we almost automatically bristle if we think someone is doing the fault-finding thing to us.

While it's become ingrained in a lot of us, I'd like to ditch the fault-finding, to be better at cutting people more slack and at seeing the good in others. I have no idea what twists and turns, good and bad, have brought them to where they are now.

Wouldn't it be just as easy, in waiting rooms and at intersections, to pick out positives instead of negatives?

Manning again: "To live and think as Jesus did is to discover the sincerity, goodness and truth often hidden behind the gross, coarse exteriors of our fellow human beings. It is to see the good in others that they don't see in themselves and to affirm this good."

I want eyes that see like that.

Enough About Me—What Do You Think of My Hat?

We make goofy videos of ourselves, launch them on You-Tube and dream about them going viral. We picture ourselves on reality shows. We make clever comments on Twitter, hoping to accumulate followers. *People* and *Us Weekly* magazines fly off our supermarket shelves. So does one called *Self.*

These days, it's all about the fame. We're determined to get famous (or to be associated with someone famous), almost no matter what it takes. Somehow the idea has taken hold that being a celebrity will complete us. If we can get recognized when we go places, life will be good.

Compare our "look at me!" need for attention with this description in the Bible of John the Baptist, a cousin of Jesus who came to announce Christ's arrival: "He himself was not the light; he came only as a witness to the light."

The world today tells us we must seek the light for ourselves. We should be in the limelight, and bask in the spotlight. Our name should be in lights. Perhaps the most sought after light we know is the one that flashes from the cameras of the paparazzi.

It wasn't long before the paparazzi of the day were trailing Jesus and when John was asked about his cousin's rapidly-growing fame, he offered another countercultural response: "He must become greater; I must become less."

What John was saying is something I believe we already know at some deep, perhaps unconscious, level: Real fulfillment and real contentment come when we're absorbed in God and others, not when we're trying to get the spotlight to shine in our direction. It's the way we're built.

One of the most contented people I know is a woman who once worked as an emergency medical technician, regularly helping people in their moments of greatest need. She is blessed with a calm, reassuring demeanor and still makes herself available to those who need her, though she no longer rides with the rescue squad. Her prospects of being famous don't look good.

I know a couple who, now that they're empty-nesters, has opened their home to young people who move to their town to study or work. Some live there, gatherings are held there, and hospitality and warmth are always served there. One of the young men who hung around the house ended up marrying their daughter. This was not reported on TMZ.com.

Another couple has dedicated their careers to working with the underprivileged. They aren't getting rich, but their house is a gathering place for both friends and strangers. They haven't made the pages of *People* yet.

One other couple are schoolteachers, the kind who get visits and notes from former students because they've poured themselves into young people. They smile a lot, but haven't yet been featured on the Today show.

Fame, like many things, is not a bad thing in itself. It can be used well, and often is. But examples of people who have mishandled it, or went astray seeking it, or got it for the wrong reasons are not hard to come by. And I think many who have received it have found fame confusing and unfulfilling.

Being a "witness to the light" seems like a whole lot better way to do life.

There's More to The Story, Part 2

"You don't really know me until you know my story," a friend recently said.

An articulate and accomplished professional and a black woman, she went on to say that parts of that story, as a child growing up in a Southern state, include having a shotgun and some profane racial epithets aimed at her by an inexplicably angry, older white man one day. Another day, she made the mistake of entering a restaurant through the front door, again as a child, and was heaped with verbal abuse by white diners.

These days, she can't help but notice the difference between the way she's sometimes treated on the job and the way her white predecessor was. She's strong, and doesn't let it affect her or the way she works.

And she's right—I didn't really know her before I knew her story.

When I think about it, I'm amazed at the number of snap judgments I can make about other people in a single day, judgments that actually have a lot more to say about me than they do about them. Every human being is living a story, an intensely personal one, and I know so few of its details.

I know a woman who lived on the next block when I was growing up. She's now in her 80s and if you met her, you'd be mightily impressed by the active lifestyle she maintains. When I was a middle-schooler, she'd play tennis with me, and today she's still out on the pickleball court, takes dance lessons and occasionally emails me jokes. If you passed her in the grocery store, you'd have no idea that she recently fought through a year-long ordeal of cancer treatments and then emerged only to find herself caring for her husband, recently diagnosed with Alzheimer's.

You wouldn't really know her until you knew her story.

If you met a guy I went to college with, you'd see a family man with a lovely and supportive wife and two sons who are growing up to become fine young men. He might show you some very cool photos of a recent scuba-diving adventure—and you wouldn't know that each year, on the anniversary of the death of his infant daughter, he quietly visits her grave.

You wouldn't really know him without knowing his story.

While a great number of us have stories marked by significant suffering, and all of us eventually will, many aren't living a story currently distinguished by its pain. If you ran across my sister, for instance, you'd see a woman who's been married for 30 years, raised three children and enjoyed a successful business career, routinely dealing with economic principles I can't even convincingly pretend to understand. But you'd have no idea she's about to embark on a four-month extravaganza of freeze-dried food and sore muscles, during which she hopes to hike the Appalachian Trail all the way from Georgia to Maine.

You wouldn't really know her until you knew her story.

"We live in narrative, we live in story. Existence has a story shape to it. We have a beginning and an end, we have a plot, and we have characters," says author Eugene Peterson.

It's true, and every day we encounter people with amazing stories. I know people who have struggled mightily with substance abuse, people who've seen war from far too close, who are raising children with disabilities or have lost a son or daughter. And I know people who have stories of unexpected accomplishment—they've climbed Mt. Kilimanjaro or won an award or saved someone's life or spend their days making life better for others. And you don't really know them until you know their stories.

Elie Wiesel, author and Nobel Peace Prize winner, has

said, "God created man because he loves stories."

We love stories, too, even though we know they don't always have happy endings. It would open both eyes and doors if we could know a bit more about the stories of those around us. We might really get to know them.

Hang Up and Drive?

One morning on the way to work, I decided to count the number of drivers passing by who were using their phones while behind the wheel. In the about 25 minutes it took to reach my office, the unofficial number hit nine, including one young lady moving rapidly about five feet behind me on the interstate who I was 92 percent certain would immediately rear-end me if I so much as tapped my brakes.

We are people easily and almost constantly distracted from what's really most important. On that particular morning, for the woman in the Toyota behind me, here's how the importance of things seemed to play out:

- Rather important: Responding to that text and, perhaps, choosing the absolute perfect emoji.
- Not terribly important: Avoiding death, destruction, blood, guts, and carnage (for both oneself and others) while behind the wheel.

There's another term for the way many of us approach

life: It's called "taking your eye off the ball," a habit of mine and just one reason my tennis career ended without the string of Wimbledon titles I'd always dreamed of.

We spend an alarming amount of time being distracted and distracting ourselves. I don't really want to spend my life caught up in the immediate and the trivial. I do, however, spend a good chunk of my time exactly that way. And I don't think I'm alone. Some of this is unavoidable, of course. We have things we have to do: there's a paycheck to be earned and countless details that need attention.

But one of my greatest fears is to find myself on my deathbed, trying my best to muster the strength to kick myself for the way I spent most of my days.

I read something recently that helps clarify my thinking about all this. "Until you know to whom, or to what, you are committed, you have not begun to live," says M. Craig Barnes, a pastor and seminary president.

He makes good sense. Without some sense of purpose about life and some commitment to that purpose, what, exactly, is the point? Which brings me back to my deathbed. It's our culture's way not to think or talk about death, including, and perhaps especially, our own. But I find that reminding myself of the fact that I'll be checking out at some point, and I that have no control over when that point arrives, is actually pretty helpful. It almost forces me to ask myself what I believe is most important—and if my life really reflects my answer.

Rick Warren, author of the mega-bestseller called, well, The Purpose-Driven Life, included these two statements in the book: "Life on earth is a temporary assignment" and "Everyone's life is driven by something." What's driving my very temporary life? Is it what I say it is?

If we lived our lives with both a clearer sense of how short they really are and a stronger focus on what makes them meaningful, how would it change us? Who would we choose to spend more time with? Less? Would we spend as much time on social media? Would we read more? Pray more? Love more freely? Fret less? Fret more?

The distractions are limitless and readily available, and it's very, very easy to become consumed with them, or on meeting our immediate needs. Here's Jesus on distractions and immediate needs: "Seek the Kingdom of God above all else, and live righteously, and he will give you everything you need." It's interesting to me that we're assured only of getting what we need.

One thing I know I need is to keep shifting my vision from the seemingly-pressing items of everyday life to the things the Apostle Paul described as "true, noble, right, pure, lovely, admirable, excellent and praiseworthy."

I'd like to get better at keeping my eye on the ball. Except maybe in traffic.

King and the King

Forty-seven years ago today, Dr. Martin Luther King, Jr. was shot and killed outside his hotel room in Memphis, Tenn. I was a third-grader living a couple hundred miles east, just outside Nashville, and the muted-but-celebratory reaction of our next-door neighbors, the ones with the George Wallace bumper stickers, is my first real memory of racism.

That April day was not the first attempt on King's life. His home had previously been the target of bombers and, in 1958, he was stabbed in the chest while doing a book-signing in New York City, suffering a wound that came within an eyelash of killing him. He was hospitalized for almost two weeks.

The looming threat of sudden, violent death shadowed King. He didn't shrink from it, once telling a crowd of supporters, "If one day you find me sprawled out dead, I do not want you to retaliate with a single act of violence. I urge you to continue protesting with the same dignity and discipline you have shown so far."

I have very significant doubts about whether I'd have the courage or conviction to press on with something I was all but certain would end in my violent death.

King did, though, and found strength not only in the justice of his cause, but in his commitment to his faith, which solidified as a young man. "I decided early to give my life to something eternal and absolute," he said. "Not to these little gods that are here today and gone tomorrow, but to God who is the same yesterday, today and forever."

Many know King's title of "Doctor," but fewer know he got it by earning a doctoral degree in theology from Boston University in 1955. Before that, he held a bachelor's divinity degree from Crozer Seminary in Pennsylvania. He was an unabashedly committed Christian and served as the pastor of churches in Alabama and Georgia.

"I would rather be a man of conviction than a man of conformity," he once said. "Occasionally in life one develops a conviction so precious and meaningful that he will stand on it till the end."

That conviction was the foundation of the man who was struck down in Memphis.

King's Christianity gave him the strength and resolve to press on when he and fellow participants in the Montgomery Bus Boycott came under attack. Urging angry residents not to retaliate, he told a crowd gathered outside his bomb-damaged home, "This is the way of Christ; it is the way of the cross. We must somehow believe that unearned suffering is redemptive."

He stood by that sentiment in the face of the inexplicable injustice that followed that string of Montgomery bombings: Seven white men were arrested for the crimes, confessed—and were acquitted anyway.

That was the man struck down in Memphis.

His understanding of the teachings of Jesus, along with a study of the tactics used by Gandhi during India's struggle for freedom, gave King his reasoning to oppose prejudice and segregation with nonviolence, even in the face of violent reprisals.

Refusing to call such an approach surrender, he instead described it as "a courageous confrontation of evil by the power of love," later adding, "I cannot make myself believe that God wanted me to hate. I'm tired of violence, I've seen too much of it…I want to rise to a higher level. We have a power that can't be found in Molotov cocktails."

Confronted by those who advocated outright armed rebellion, King preached reconciliation instead. After a sit-in, he said, "Our ultimate aim was not to defeat or humiliate the white man, but to win his friendship and understanding. We had a moral obligation to remind him that segregation is wrong. We protested with the ultimate aim of being reconciled with our white brothers."

That was the man who died so violently in Memphis.

This, however, must also be said: While King was undeniably courageous and committed, he was also human, imperfect and flawed like the rest of us. Some of his flaws have been well-documented in the years since his death. And King, like everyone else, didn't brag about this. But he knew it well enough not to encourage the image of sainthood among his followers.

"I want you to know I'm a sinner like all of God's children," he said, the day before he died. "But I want to be a good man…Every time you set out to be good, there's something pulling on you, telling you to be evil. Every time you set out to love, something keeps pulling on you, trying to get you to hate…all of us know somehow that there is a Mr. Hyde and a Dr. Jekyll in us."

That, too, is the man who died on the balcony of his hotel in Memphis. It sure would have been nice to have had him around for a while longer.

Rolling Uphill

The hotel is just blocks from the White House and features a spectacular 12-story atrium lobby, topped with a glass roof. But every time I hung out in that enormous lobby during my two-day stay, all I could really see was the people.

I was there for a conference focusing on the challenges faced by people with physical disabilities as they live independent lives and, as a non-disabled person, the buzz of activity in the lobby was stunning. People criss-crossed the shiny floors in wheelchairs, both motorized and self-powered; others tapped their way with white canes, wearing dark glasses, and sometimes had someone to help guide them. Some went past using crutches and canes; others had misshapen limbs. Most spoke easily and clearly; others needed someone accustomed to hearing their speech to translate for them.

It's not out of the ordinary to encounter someone with a disability, but seeing a couple hundred such individuals in one place stopped me short.

A conversation from the Old Testament found its way into my head. In it, God is recorded telling Samuel, "Do not consider his appearance or his height...The Lord does not look at the things people look at. People look at the outward appearance, but the Lord looks at the heart."

If only we could learn to do that. The folks who attended this conference are people who live life every day being judged by their appearance, to an even greater degree than the rest of us do. They're quite aware that others are making assumptions about them wherever they go.

"You can often see people thinking, 'Uh-oh, what do I do now?' when I arrive," says my friend Kelly, who has used a wheelchair her whole life, "and sometimes you can feel their expectations just sort of dropping."

That's so misguided, because Kelly is one of the most

competent people I know. Don't call her, or anyone else, "disabled people." They're not at all disabled as people, as individuals, any more than anyone else is. Their humanity is unaffected; they just must wear a part of their imperfection in a more obvious way than most of us do. They are "people with physical disabilities." They're beloved sons and daughters of God, and very often searching for opportunities to have real relationships with people willing to see them the same way they see anyone else.

In that regard, they are completely and totally the same as every other human on the planet. You. Me.

They're also not alone, unfortunately, in going through life constantly enduring the judgments of others based on the way they look. Think for a minute, for example, what it must be like to be obese in today's world. How might that feel when you walk into a room for the first time? What if there's some unmistakable sign of poverty in the way you dress? How self-conscious might that make you feel?

Or, of course, to be an individual who feels noticed and labeled because of his or her race. We don't have to work too hard to find examples of how that can play out.

What an injustice we do to a person when we assume something about them based on their appearance. We know enough not to do that to ourselves--we understand very well that we're made up of so much more than the way we look. Our looks are not what make us who we really are.

It's not just unfair and wrong to decide something about someone because of the way they look—it's lazy. It's a shortcut we can use to avoid actually getting to know someone. It saves us the trouble of entering into an authentic relationship, even if just for a brief time.

If being reminded of that is the only thing I end up taking away from being at this conference, it was time well spent.

Appreciate That, Jesus

Life inside my comfort zone can be pretty easy. I get used to it, and things go fairly smoothly most of the time. A lot of us live a lot of life that way.

From what I can tell, Jesus pretty much hates comfort zones. And I don't mean to be flippant or disrespectful about someone I profess to follow, but this can be downright annoying. Jesus has this habit of speaking the truth-- the whole truth, all the time—and challenging me with it, sometimes gently, sometimes not so much.

I'm not a big fan of being confronted, especially when the confronter is so obviously right. And few things can be as uncomfortable as the truth.

For example: I try my best not to dislike people, but sometimes it just doesn't work out. There are some folks in my life I feel pretty comfortable disliking: they're domineering, or spend most of our conversations trying to be sure I know how important they are, or just flat-out grating. I tend to avoid these people and, when I can't, I can be a tad short with them. I'm sure they pick up on it sometimes.

So here's Jesus: "If you are kind only to your friends, how are you different from anyone else? If you love only those who love you, what reward is there for that?"

Um, thanks for that, Jesus.

Also, I'm an adult. I have a job and a family, and I like to set my own priorities. That's not unique: Who doesn't want the illusion of feeling in control of their own lives, to be, as a friend recently put it, "the star of our own movie"?

Jesus isn't comfortable with this. "If anyone would come after me," he says, "he must deny himself and take up his cross daily and follow me." And, "What good is it for a man to gain the whole world and yet lose his very self?"

My level of discomfort is creeping up, Jesus.

When I feel someone has treated me badly, it can be

really, really hard to forgive them, put it behind me and move on. It can be comfortably satisfying to feel like the wronged party, the victim of an injustice. And often, the doer of the allegedly bad deed doesn't even know or care if I forgive them or not, so why do it?

There are probably several good reasons, but here's Jesus again, in the prayer He taught His disciples, the prayer so many of us pray so often: "Forgive us our sins as we forgive those who sin against us."

That's really the way it works, Jesus? I can't just get my forgiveness while also enjoying my grudges? Not cool. Not cool at all.

I usually try to do the right thing. I do my best to keep the Commandments, to be kind to people, and to help out when I can. Also, I haven't held up any convenience stores lately. I do speed sometimes, though. This is pretty exemplary stuff, right, Jesus?

Jesus: "I tell you that unless your righteousness surpasses that of the Pharisees and the teachers of the law, you will certainly not enter the kingdom of heaven."

He's talking about the revered church leaders of his time. OK, many of them were serious hypocrites, but who among us sometimes isn't? I think He might be telling me I'm not going to be able to do this alone.

This is not comforting, Jesus.

Jesus said a lot of things during His time here. Some of them are very comforting, and even unbelievably inspiring. However, some are also very unsettling and not at all comfortable. But I believe everything he said is also one other thing—true.

And it's also clear, looking back, that Jesus has always had my best interests at heart. So in my clearest moments, I can admit that almost all the best things that happen in my life happen when I'm outside my comfort zone.

Mark Twain may have had it right when he said, "It ain't those parts of the Bible I can't understand that bother me, it's the parts I do understand."

Our Helpless God?

It was a spectacular late morning and a beautiful drive down Grove Avenue with the sunroof open, on the way to lunch—and then suddenly it was one of the most frightening moments I can remember.

Looking across the median I saw a beautiful little dark-haired girl, probably about four years old, wandering across a side street alone. Some kind of stuffed animal in hand, she had to be within 10 feet or so of the 35-mile-per-hour, four-lane traffic passing by on Grove. Any driver who made a right turn onto that side street would have needed the reflexes of an Indy driver to avoid hitting her.

The little girl looked like she might have been crossing from one small group of family members or friends to another, because there were a few adults and other children on both sides of the street. But she and her stuffed animal were making that crossing all by themselves.

I'm not sure I've ever gripped a steering wheel that hard. It was an awful, painful feeling that made my stomach hurt immediately--and this pretty little girl was a stranger's child. I can't imagine what it might have felt like if she'd been either of my two daughters. It hurts just to type that.

I think it's a feeling God can imagine very well.

He sees his sons and daughters in harm's way every day—every waking moment (and the Bible says he "neither slumbers nor sleeps").

It's not a perfect analogy because this little girl didn't intentionally do anything wrong (and she did cross safely), but I drove away thinking about the day I heard a speaker use this very powerful line: "God hates sin the way a mother hates the disease that's killing her child." That was a perspective-changer for me. For God, it must be a similar kind of sickening, helpless and yes, even scary, feeling when He sees His children make mistakes that put them in harm's way.

Many of us have heard plenty about God's anger over things we do wrong, but we haven't heard as much about this: it's clear that He grieves over our wrongdoing, too. It causes Him to suffer. In Genesis, it says, "The Lord observed the extent of human wickedness on the earth, and… it broke his heart." Later, the prophet Isaiah was speaking of Jesus, who would come centuries later, when he said, "It was our weaknesses he carried; it was our sorrows that weighed him down."

God must get a pretty awful feeling, for instance, when He sees one of His sons taking something that's not His, or when one of His daughters willfully does something she knows is wrong. He knows the pain we're bringing on ourselves. No one wants to watch his kids get hurt.

It must bring Him sadness when His children spread unkind rumors and gossip about some of His other children.

He must hurt when He sees the things we sometimes do to each other, the things we sometimes say to each other, and all the ways we find to hurt each other. And then there's the horrific violence and abuse we're sometimes capable of.

He must grieve when we put our needs and desires above those of everyone else around us.

The point here is not that to make anyone feel guilty about ruining God's day. I just think it can be helpful to try this perspective on at times: If there's a God who created me, loves me and has done more for me than I can describe, and who then suffers when I do Him and His children wrong, why would I want to make Him feel that way? And, as Mother Teresa once said, "Why stoop down to things that will spoil the beauty of our hearts?"

And one final question: Why can't we do a better job of helping each other through life's dangerous intersections?

Was It Something I Ate?

I was going to be the one who did all the right things, the one that dodged the bullet that is the cardiovascular health history of the Allen men. I exercised, didn't smoke, took my Lipitor, and tried to keep my intake of chocolate ice cream at something less than gluttonous levels.

Man plans and God laughs, goes an old Yiddish proverb.

This is not to say that God got a good chuckle out of my recent medical adventure. I'd bet against that. But I'm thinking He would have no objection if I take it as a reminder of just how little I actually can control in life and, maybe, a chance to think again about how I spend each of my days.

One Monday morning, as I drove to work, the pressure in my chest grew, no matter how much I attempted to burp it away. I'd had pressure before, plenty of times, and the burping usually took care of it. But then a pain went down my right side. I hadn't had that before. "Heart attack pain isn't on the right," I reassured myself. "It's in the middle of the chest, on the left side, down the left arm or up the neck." I've read the brochures.

I made it to the office, whereupon a co-worker pronounced, "You look green." Green is not my natural color and, since it felt like a pretty good description of how I was feeling, I agreed to let her drive me to the hospital, where my wife met me (I couldn't bring myself to call 911 at the office—didn't want any of my colleagues to fall behind in their work, you know. Medical types will tell you that this was unwise.).

By the end of the day, I had a brand-new stent on board, a little, spring-like piece of metal that's supposed to keep open the 80 percent blockage I had in the heart artery known in medical circles as the "widow-maker."

"Did I have a heart attack?" I asked the cardiologist. He shook his head. "You had a heart 'event,'" he said.

Not long after, my wife, Cathy, and I were watching TV and one of those pharmaceutical ads came on where at the end they list all the possible side effects of the drug, such as minor nausea and/or painful death. The announcer said it was not for people who had a "heart condition." I asked Cathy, a nurse, if that meant me. Yup, after only 54 trips around the sun, I officially had a heart condition.

The whole thing has been kind of a surreal experience and, as I try to understand and live it, I've wondered what God would have me take away from it.

Maybe, at least in part, this: One of my favorite things Jesus ever said was, "I have come that you might have life, and have it to the full."

I want my life to be more "full" now. In a very real way, every day that we wake up is a gift. I heard it said once, "What did you trade your 24 hours of life for today?"

Jesus, I'm sure, meant a bunch of things when he said "full," but perhaps one of them is that we live in such a way that each day means something. It's very trendy to say we "live in the moment." That expression may be getting a little shopworn—but sometimes the truth can feel that way, because in some cases we've heard it all our lives. We may need to discover it anew. In the end, "in the moment" is probably the healthiest way we can live. I want to do more for, and with, people. I think I'll look at the sky more often.

Quirky author Anne Lamott was in town to speak recently and at one point, she quoted a fellow quirky author: "E.L. Doctorow once said, 'Writing a novel is like driving a car at night. You can see only as far as your headlights, but you can make the whole trip that way.' This is right up there with the best advice on writing, or life, I have ever heard."

So is this, from a wise friend of mine named Jason. A couple weeks after I left the hospital, he asked me how I was feeling. I told him things were pretty much back to normal. "Glad to hear it," he said, "but don't lose that sense of appreciation for life that a scare like that gives you."

I'm trying.

Me, Too

A few years ago, my friend's divorce became final. There were, as usual, extenuating circumstances. And the whole process was, as usual, excruciating and emotionally draining. Today, the couple's children have adjusted to shared custody and new living arrangements as best they can, and the ex-spouses are moving on, also as best they can.

After the divorce, my friend met someone who was fun to be with and who treated her well. They began dating, and did so for more than a year. He was also divorced, and together they explored what it means to experience and enjoy a relationship again, territory fraught with challenges for both of them.

One Sunday, the two of them showed up at my friend's church. While there were smiles and pleasantries all around, eyebrows went up.

"Did you see her?" one woman in the congregation asked another.

"Oh, yes," said the second woman, eyes rolling, "and she's with that new guy."

Fortunately, my friend knows nothing of this conversation, although she was certainly not oblivious to some of the sentiments that morning. She's not been back.

Her experience brings to mind an incident related by writer Philip Yancey. A Chicago prostitute found herself homeless, sick and unable to buy food. In desperation, she turned to a friend of Yancey's who, among other things, suggested she go to a church for help.

"Church?!" she responded, shocked. "Why would I ever go there? I was already feeling terrible about myself. They'd just make me feel worse."

I'm in no way equating my friend's situation to that of the prostitute. But having said that, what's going on here? If any buildings in the world ought to have a welcome mat

out front, shouldn't it be church buildings? If you're desperate and hurting, shouldn't you be able to find refuge and
acceptance in a church, whether or not you call yourself a
person of faith?

Why is this so often not the case? Does the fact that
I may attend church services and may consider myself a
"good person" make me, in any way, superior to someone
who doesn't? What if that other person's marriage has fallen
apart? What if she or he is a prostitute? Do I have any right
to be anything short of welcoming to anyone who walks
through the door of my church? Or the doors of my life?

No, I do not.

I am a Christian, but my faith certainly hasn't, by a
long shot, cornered the market on this whole acceptance
business. Christians gather as a church in the name of Jesus.
Think for a minute about who His pals were. His closest
female friend had been a prostitute, and among His group
of close male friends were a despised tax collector and a
thief who would later help get Him killed. He had interactions with a woman of an unpopular minority group who
had been through five husbands, another woman caught in
adultery, lepers, pagans and various outcasts. Jesus never
made them feel anything less than accepted—special, even.

Maybe we're all prostitutes. And divorcees. And you
name it. We all have our secret—and not so secret—sins.
We know we've messed it up, sometimes in a big way.
Deep down, whether we'll admit it to anyone else or not,
we sense our need to be forgiven—for things we've done,
said and thought, and just for being the way we sometimes are.

We want to feel clean. And free.

Can we want anything less for others?

Me, Too, Part 2: Carolyn

A while back, I wrote that if a person feels unwelcome just about everywhere else in the world, he or she should always be made to feel welcome by the people of a church. That should be the way love works.

A few days later, I received an e-mail from a man I didn't know. It began, "Everything you are about to read is true."

He went on to tell the story of a 26-year-old friend who was making some poor life choices and also had developed a prescription drug problem, and wondered if I would help him find a church that could help her "begin the difficult process of trying to turn her life around."

Some of what he went on to say seemed a bit difficult to swallow, but here's what convinced me that his story must be true: At one point, he wrote, "For reasons I won't go into here (but you will be able to surmise, I suspect), I cannot take her in myself."

That sounded so human, so very like the difficult situations we allow ourselves to get into.

I think what he was really asking was if anything I'd written was actually true. Can hope truly be found through a community of people trying to live their faith? Or is a church just a building where people get together to be seen, socialize and mouth nice words?

Is there a God, and if so, does it make any difference in the lives of those who profess to believe in Him? And if it does, what can they offer to someone whose life has come to a very precarious place?

All of us are broken, in ways known only to ourselves and maybe to a few people close to us. I haven't met any exceptions yet. This young woman's brokenness was just harder to hide. And she, like everyone else, was in desperate need of someone to welcome her in that brokenness, and thereby help to heal it.

In subsequent e-mails over the next couple weeks, this man offered more details about the obstacles his friend was facing and how some of the places she'd turned for help just seemed to create more of them. He was doing what he could.

Friends had steered me in the direction of one local church that seemed especially able and willing to step in, and I'd had a chance to speak with a staff member there who'd been down some of the same roads this young woman was navigating. She was delightful, and eager to help.

The church and the e-mailer had each other's contact information, and I think he was beginning to feel some optimism about the future for his friend. So, when he sent me another e-mail a little over a week later, I eagerly opened it to get the update.

It was a copy of his friend's obituary.

"I wish I had done more sooner to try to get her more help," he wrote. "I know in my heart that she is with God now… I will miss her forever," ending with, "May God bless all our souls."

He wasn't entirely sure of her cause of death, but thought it likely that it was a drug overdose.

I very much wish that this story had ended differently, and I very much wish that I could come up with an explanation as to why it didn't. I can't.

I can only offer this: One of the reasons we're here is to help each other. We've got to keep getting better at it.

And this: "He tends his flock like a shepherd; He gathers the lambs in his arms and carries them close to his heart" (Isaiah 40:11). Despite the way this story ended, I believe that this particular lamb was always close to His heart, and remains there.

Beggars and Choosers

Depending on the route I take to and from the office on a typical weekday, I can come face to face with anywhere from one or two to as many as seven or eight down-on-their-luck people, panhandling at traffic lights.

Some are older and look a bit grizzled and worn from their time on the streets. Others are young and wear looks of defeat and resignation you don't usually see on people their age. Some are women; most are men. This time of year, all are cold.

Occasionally, some are a bit aggressive, like the man on the Boulevard who approached my semi-open window one afternoon and barked, "Come on, man! Do you think I really want to beg?"

Their cardboard signs advertise their hard times, their unemployment, and even their ex-military status, but mostly their badly damaged hopes.

What's a person of faith supposed to do with this? How do I live my beliefs, idling at an intersection in a warm car, as a fellow human being stands just a few feet away, clearly asking for help?

Two of the things I love that Jesus said are, "Freely you have received; freely give," and "Whatsoever you do for the least of these, you do for me." Caring for those less fortunate than we are is a central tenet of every major faith out there. Doing so feels right, and good.

But I can't feel right and good every time I hit a red light at Belvidere and Cary. And I'm not sure I should. Most social service agencies, plus a good friend who is a long-time social worker, say you shouldn't give to panhandlers, that Richmond has plenty of well-publicized services for the homeless.

For a long time, I've used that advice as my "get out of jail free" card, falling back on it at traffic lights all over the city. But when I think about it, why does it feel like a relief to get such permission? Why would I not want to give to someone desperate enough to swallow their pride, grab a sign and stand out in the cold at an intersection?

I understand that there are perfectly legitimate an-swers to that question, but, as I wait for the light to change, it often still feels like a lack of compassion. Panhandling, like many issues, looks different when there's a face on it.

Some will say that money given to a panhandler will probably just end up being misspent anyway, perhaps to feed an addiction of some kind. That may be true, but should that be a major part of my decision-making? If I give a guy a couple bucks, does that buy me the right to tell him how to spend it? He's a grownup and it's now his money.

Maybe what's more important are my motives for giv-ing: The transaction is between him and me, but it's also between Him and me. If I give a panhandler something because I feel a nudge from God to do so, shouldn't that be enough for me? How the recipient of the cash spends it depends on whatever nudges he may or may not feel. Does that make me irresponsible?

To be honest, I keep my window rolled up most of the time. That's partly because if I give away money at ev-ery intersection, it's going to cost me a significant chunk of change. And partly because I'm not sure it's the best way to truly help people in need. And, frankly, partly because sometimes I just don't want to part with my money.

Years ago, I met a woman who ran a homeless shelter in Fredericksburg. As I sat in her office and watched her interact with the men, women and children coming and going from the sleeping areas and kitchen, she told me about some of their hard-luck stories and bad decisions. "A lot of people look down on these folks, but you know what?" she said. "We're all God's children."

Maybe that's why, even though I know a little about what's available for the sign-holders at Richmond intersections, it can still feel so strange to drive by them.

Yeah, But is it True?

I have this clear memory from the mostly-foggy years of my early childhood. I'm with my oldest sister, in the living room of our family's home in upstate New York. I couldn't have been more than five, which means she couldn't have been more than four.

We were sitting on the floor behind a large chair and a small end table, just passing some time by sticking our fingers into an electrical outlet in the wall. (Please don't hold this against my parents—child-proofing homes was not yet in vogue.)

I don't remember if we were actually getting shocked, but I do know that something didn't feel especially good. Being the older and clearly wiser of the two of us, I explained to my sister that the pain we were feeling was caused by a very small animal inside the outlet who was sticking us with a pin. She's a bit smarter these days (master's degree and all), but back then she bought my explanation.

It wasn't the truth.

Neither did I encounter the truth during a recent quest to straighten out a small financial matter with my bank. I thought I could fix everything on the bank's website, so I went online and was offered a chance to computer-chat with a customer service person. I took it and was quickly connected with "Suzy Davidson," who promised to be most helpful.

However, the English she typed during our conversation was so stilted and peculiar that about halfway into it I asked, "Are you a computer?" She quickly typed back, assuring me she was an actual human. So we continued, and were able to decipher one another well enough to arrive at a solution to my problem.

As we typed our goodbyes, I asked her where she was based. "I am bank associate located in India," she responded. She couldn't hear me chuckle, but if her name is really Suzy Davidson, then mine is Mahatma Gandhi.

It wasn't the truth.

Granted, these are a couple of pretty minor instances of people messing with the truth. But the reason we notice when someone does that is that truth is not a minor thing. It's a very big deal—in the end, truth may well be the only thing.

We're all looking for it, at some level, whether we acknowledge it or not. Some of us make an honest search for truth as we live our lives; some of us cobble together a kind of truth that makes us comfortable and mostly satisfied; and some of us accept what we've always been told as truth, without much questioning.

The search gets a little sticky, for me and for lots of people, because of the nature of truth. If something really is true, then it's true whether I like it or not. Truth doesn't get put to the popular vote. I don't believe the power to determine ultimate truth is mine; nor is the option to create a kind of personal truth that makes me happy.

For both my life here on this planet and for the life that I believe follows, the truth matters, and I think the search for it is one of the reasons we're here. Some of history's great thinkers have put a very high priority on that search:

Henry David Thoreau penned, "Rather than love, than money, than fame, give me truth."

"The pursuit of truth and beauty is a sphere of activity in which we are permitted to remain children all our lives," said Albert Einstein.

There are few activities more worth the investment of our time. And few that will have a larger impact on our lives. We should be all-in for it.

As for me, I have great respect for the words of Thoreau, Einstein and others. I'll continue to live my own search, with all its stops, starts, side trips, doubts and occasional insights. That search has led me to the words of an itinerant preacher and carpenter, a Jewish man from the Middle East named Jesus. He said, "If you hold to my teachings, you are really my disciples. Then you will know the truth, and the truth will set you free."

Toby's Tale

Toby died early one June and, to my way of thinking, much too early in life. He was 52, and he was alone.

We met 30-some years ago, when fate brought us together in Richmond as college freshmen and roommates. I was a Catholic Yankee; he was a good Southern Baptist. He was one of the first people my own age I'd ever met who seemed to think that his faith should be the guiding force of his life. He was serious about it, involved in church activities and community service projects and even, on some occasions, asked to preach at a local church, which was stunning to me.

When we graduated from college, Toby signed on with what was then the Southern Baptist Foreign Mission Board and spent two years doing missionary work in Kenya. Later he enrolled in a seminary in California to pursue a career in the ministry.

Not long after he began his studies, my wife and I were in San Diego and Toby came to spend a couple days with us there, wowing us by ferrying us around town in his rented Lincoln Town Car. That's when he first told me that he was gay.

Several years later, after he'd quit seminary and gone into the business world, Toby came to visit and wowed my children by ferrying them around town in his rented convertible. That's when he first told me that he was HIV-positive.

He returned to the West Coast, and the next decade or so became a slow, downward spiral into substance abuse, depression and a host of serious physical ailments. He became too unhealthy to work, lived on disability benefits, and ended up as one of the youngest residents of a Bay Area assisted-living facility.

At various points, I figured his dire circumstances and

the disapproval he'd received from many had caused him to leave his faith behind, but he insisted that he remained a Christian and continued attending services and reading the Bible.

I'd like to think that I could have done the same, but I really don't know.

It's easy to wonder where God was in all this. Toby had to feel, at least sometimes, that he'd gotten a pretty lousy deal from the Almighty. We were friends for years, so he knew my loving and supportive parents and siblings; he, on the other hand, lost his father as an elementary school student and, not long after, saw his mother institutionalized and unable to care for him for some time. I remember family vacations; Toby remembers his mother sitting in a car with him, trying to decide whether to drive them both off a dock and into a river. There's lots more.

Why did Toby have to face such trauma and so many obstacles? And why did I not have to? What was God doing with all this? What was Toby supposed to be learning? What was I?

The questions are easy to come by; answers are not. As is often the case with the things of God, the only answer seems to be that we just don't know. We must make room for mystery. I can't explain why Toby faced the circumstances he did, or why he lived the life he did. I do know that he struggled mightily and suffered much. Sometimes, part of what God seems to ask of us, including Toby and including me, is the courage to accept what comes our way without necessarily understanding why, and to press on anyway. That kind of trust can be awful hard to come by.

Toby struggled for that trust and lived in that mystery more than many of us have, I think, stubbornly believing in a God who loved him. I'd like to think he's seeing the fruit of that belief today.

The Wheels Come Off
in the Motor City

We were headed for Detroit, a good 10-hour road trip, and I'd been so impressed with our efficiency. We'd never been there—nor really planned to go—but our nephew had decided he'd marry a Motor City girl and we didn't want to miss the big event.

Our plan was to leave Richmond at 2:30 in the morning so we'd get there in time to pick up our son and daughter at the Detroit airport. So my wife, youngest daughter and I successfully dragged ourselves up in the middle of the night, loaded the suitcases into the car, and actually left a few minutes early.

That's the part I was impressed with.

Everything went smoothly, we found the airport, and we even had a little time to check out downtown Detroit, where we looked across the water at Canada, a faraway land we couldn't visit because my passport is expired. At the hotel, as I unloaded, I looked around and had a semi-troubling thought.

"Isn't there supposed to be a garment bag?" I asked my wife, trying to be casual, like maybe it really hadn't been my responsibility to load the car in the wee hours that morning.

Yes, indeed there was supposed to a garment bag, one that contained my suit, her dress and the youngest daughter's dress for the wedding. In the quiet moment immediately following my question, I saw the somewhat pained expression on my wife's face and realized where the garment bag was: still hanging in a closet several states and many hours to the southeast.

The wedding was less than 24 hours away, and we were looking at the possibility of an emergency shopping spree that could do unnecessary and unexpected damage to the magnetic strip on my credit card. This was not good, especially since I make it a policy to wear a suit as infrequently as possible and therefore only own one that fits.

My sister, mother of the groom, graciously told us not to fret and to just wear whatever other clothes we'd brought along, but I couldn't get too excited about us being the only ones at the wedding in jeans. I figured this probably wouldn't please the bride's family, either, and we'd never met any of them. Since the chances that we'll see them again at some point are pretty good, there didn't seem to be any point in riling them up right from the start.

So the shopping excursion commenced after breakfast the next morning, several hours before the 2:30 kickoff of the wedding ceremony. Did I mention how much I love Detroit? It is clearly a city that oozes grace. Within a mile of our hotel, we came upon the biggest Salvation Army store I'd ever seen, hands-down. It was huge, chock-full of appropriate wedding attire (I was pretty sure), and it immediately called to me much more insistently than would have any pricey department store we might have found. Done. Minutes later, we were wandering the racks looking over some of Michigan's finest castoff clothing.

We'd brought along our other daughter and our son as fashion consultants, who were assisted outside the fitting rooms by an amused local couple who'd observed our situation. Together, we closed the deal in about a half-hour. For $30, we walked out with dresses for my wife and daughter and a pair of pants and shirt for me (my son had brought along an extra tie).

Further, and I say this in all humility, we were stunning at the festivities that afternoon. My wife found a red dress that she looked so good in I'm pretty certain she deflected some attention from the bride. She's keeping it. I'm keeping my shirt. My pants were, well, just a bit short--but there was enough drinking at the reception I'm thinking no one really noticed. My daughter was the least pleased, though she looked great in her floral pattern dress.

Also part of the upside to all this: We felt approximately zero pressure to make sure we didn't spill anything on ourselves, which is often a concern of mine.

Upon our return, the garment bag was serenely in place, right where I'd left it. We didn't bother to unpack it for a while.

I'd go back to Detroit anytime. And pack light.

The End of the Affair, Part 1

There's a site on the Internet I won't name here, but its slogan is, "Life is short. Have an affair." The website bills itself as "the world's largest married dating service for discreet encounters," and it helps married people meet up with other married people for the sole purpose of breaking their wedding vows.

It currently claims more than 25 million "anonymous members."

One of America's largest networks has a series called "Mistresses" in its lineup. The show's website describes it as the story of "four friends [who] find support and guidance with each other as they brave their turbulent journeys and life's storms of excitement, secrecy and betrayal." Sounds like fun, doesn't it?

Maybe, but hold on a second: Whether it's attractively presented as an exciting way to connect with new "friends" online, or as entertainment in the form of a popular TV series, isn't what we're talking about here just plain old adultery? And isn't that a bad thing?

Isn't there a Commandment specifically covering this topic?

I'm not interested in pointing a finger at anyone who's ever had an extramarital affair. Some very well-meaning people I know, including some I hold near and dear, have done so. I understand the lure of the forbidden and the longing for something new and exciting. I also know that marriages invariably look different from the inside than they do from outside. People give in to temptation--it's real life.

But adultery's commonness doesn't make it OK. And it's exactly that "real life" element that's missing from the extramarital relationships that show up in many of our movies, books, songs and TV shows and on our computer screens. I'm betting the "married dating" website doesn't feature a section about the life-changing pain inflicted on the betrayed spouse and bewildered children. And I haven't seen a whole lot of TV shows and movies that glamorize the emotional upheaval left in adultery's wake. That's not "must-see TV."

The Commandment "You shall not commit adultery" wasn't given to us by a buzzkill God looking to ruin all our fun. Just the opposite, actually—I think it comes from a loving God who wants to protect the hearts and relationships of His children. He has made the relationship between a husband and a wife the most important one on earth, both to demonstrate how much He loves us and to show us that real love means putting others first.

"In sharp contrast with our culture, the Bible teaches that the essence of marriage is a sacrificial commitment to the good of the other," writes New York City pastor Tim Keller, in his book The Meaning of Marriage.

Adultery has nothing to do with the "good of the other." And it inevitably makes a mess. The marriages of at least a dozen people I know have suffered from extramarital affairs. Of those, I can think of only two couples who managed to find their way back to semi-solid footing and kept their families intact, albeit with a new sense of wariness.

Maybe we've taken some of the sting out of adultery by going easy on it semantically--it's just an "affair" or a bit of "cheating." Cheating makes it sound like you slipped an ace up your sleeve at the monthly poker game. But the stakes here are actually much higher. Adultery is an ultimate breach of trust, the breaking of a sacred promise. In our hearts, we know it's wrong: When's the last time someone got caught in an extramarital relationship and was proud of it? And why is it that we even say he or she "got caught"?

I just wish it wasn't made to look like such carefree fun in so much of our entertainment. Like violence in the media, we've become largely desensitized to it—and there are some things we shouldn't ever get desensitized to.

No website developer, actor or singer's job description calls for them to use their work to promote marriage and commitment. First Amendment rights are precious here, all the more so because those rights are so often trampled in other parts of the world. In the end, the responsibility is mine. I must be the judge of what I accept as entertainment, and how I let it subtly change me--because I believe, over time, it will.

The End of the Affair, Part 2

About a year ago, I mentioned an adultery-promoting website without naming it specifically, alluding to it only by its slogan: "Life is short. Have an affair." I used the site as an example and was hoping not to give it any extra, undeserved attention.

No need for attempts at such discretion any longer. This month, thanks to a widely-publicized computer hack, nearly everybody learned the site's name: Ashley Madison has officially hit the fan.

Lots of other names are out there now, too. We're hearing about celebrities and politicians who may be on the site, government workers using it while on the job, divorce rumors, widespread opportunities for blackmail—and it's only going to get worse. Men and women everywhere (the site claims more than 30 million users) are sweating each time they check their email.

In the aftermath of all this, the immediate temptation is to make jokes and even to gloat a little, believing a bunch of cheaters are getting what they deserve. Late-night comedians will have a field day, and I'm sure it will be hilarious. Some people of faith will point to the Bible's statement about reaping what we sow.

While the reaping and sowing thing is certainly true, I'm doing my best to resist the laughing and gloating, for a couple reasons. One is that I follow a God who I believe always stands ready to extend us grace and mercy. All of us are somehow broken and on occasion do things we know aren't really in our best interests, and all of us have secrets we would hate to have trumpeted on the Internet.

We ought not, however, be shocked when our secrets do find their way into the light. Speaking of hypocrisy, Jesus once said, "There is nothing concealed that will not be disclosed, or hidden that will not be made known.

What you have said in the dark will be heard in the day-light." And who among us isn't, at least sometimes, a bit of a hypocrite?

Another reason I don't feel equipped to start chuckling and gloating is that I think I understand at least a little of what people who commit adultery are looking for. They're after excitement, adventure and something or someone to make them feel alive and wonderful. They want a spring in their step and a reason to get up in the morning. Who doesn't?

Maybe a thrilling stroll outside of one's marriage vows can provide that for a while. But here's where it all breaks down: We're looking for something in places where it won't ever be found. It can't. We can't put our needs for fulfill-ment and joy on any other human being. No one we know, or will ever meet, can make us into the best version of ourselves. That sort of effort is always doomed to failure.

Religious thinkers have taught for centuries that only an encounter with God can free us to be who we're meant to be; only the divine can satisfy our inborn need for joy and affirmation. However, for most of us life has been a steady pursuit of other ways to fulfill that desire.

Nothing will.

"Every man who knocks on the door of a brothel is looking for God," said G.K. Chesterton, an English writer of the early 1900s, in what today seems a particularly apt assessment for the men and women of Ashley Madison.

Fifteen centuries earlier, Christian philosopher Augus-tine of Hippo wrote, "You have made us for yourself, O Lord, and our hearts are restless until they rest in you."

Part of the original equipment installed in us humans is a deep desire for something we can't quite describe, a passion for not just life, but purpose and even exhilaration, too. I'm trying my best to let the whole Ashley Madison mess serve as a reminder of where to go looking for it.

A Life-Giving 12-Pack

Over the past few years, I've developed a growing respect for the frightening power of addiction. People I know and care about have lost their marriages, derailed their careers and, in one case, even cut short their life, all because they couldn't get out from under their dependence on various substances or habits.

Addiction, no matter what its focus, is a beast that can put a stranglehold on you in a hurry. And that beast, it seems, is almost always too big for a person to tackle alone.

In 12-step groups, I'd heard that people banded to-gether to confront the beast and to learn not to be afraid of it. I wanted to see that, to see recovery as it happened. So when a friend invited me to accompany him to a 12-step meeting, I signed on.

It was a men's-only meeting, a group of guys who gather weekly to stare down the power of addiction with the most effective weapons they can muster—honesty, transparency, unity, and an utter surrender to and reliance upon God.

As we approached the meeting room, in all honesty, I had a couple of hesitant thoughts: What if I saw someone there I knew and he was embarrassed to have me know he's an addict? Or the reverse—what if someone I knew saw me and assumed I was one?

What I learned, at least in this particular meeting, is that no one seemed embarrassed about anything. There wasn't time for that—it would only hinder what they were trying to accomplish. In a room of around 25 men, from re-tirees to a teenager or two, there was no telling how many broken marriages, lost jobs, arrests and other setbacks there had been.

Except that there was telling. It was one of the most honest sharing of struggles I'd ever witnessed. Everyone there knew what it was like to drive their lives off a cliff, and each was willing to own the fallout of those disasters.

People may forever debate whether addiction should be thought of as a disease or as a personal weakness, but in this 12-step group (and, I suspect, in most), that debate was not on the table. I think if I'd asked that question, the response would have been something like, "We couldn't care less how you got here. What we do care about is moving forward—together. We can do this."

As part of the 12 steps, participants admit that they've become unable to manage their addiction and, therefore, their lives, and make a decision to seek strength from one another and from God, "as we understood him."

I don't know how each man in that room understood God, but the face they put on him was beautiful. It sure looked a lot like faith in action, and the church as the church is supposed to be. I saw no pretense, or any attempts to avoid letting others see the brokenness inside. Instead, these men acknowledged that brokenness is something we all share; offered each other unconditional acceptance, support and encouragement; and expressed a desire to make the journey toward wholeness together.

If only more of our congregations today could do the same thing.

Does that mean everyone at that meeting is on his way to a happy ending? Probably not. Every man there, along with the rest of us, know there are no guarantees and that sometimes, after years of struggle, the beast still wins. But, just by being there, the men in that room were saying that they were looking to overcome and wouldn't go down without a fight. And that they weren't willing to let their comrades do so, either.

It was a sacred space.

Superheroes in Our Midst

All four of us were in a pretty tight spot.

Michelle was pregnant with her fourth child at age 31. She had custody of only one of the other three and was trying hard to kick a stubborn heroin habit. The father of her new baby had recently become physically abusive.

Julian was 36 and just out of prison after serving time for drug distribution. He wanted desperately to reconcile with his former wife, but his history of spousal abuse was making that difficult. Adding to that difficulty was the fact that she was living with another man, who was also abusive to her.

Ella had aged out of the foster care system at 18 and ended up moving in with her boyfriend, with whom she'd since had two children. He had begun abusing her and had gotten her fired from her job by showing up at her workplace and harassing her.

I had two children with my girlfriend, who was now incarcerated. The kids stayed with my mom but she had died recently, so now they were suddenly with me. I'd been staying with friends but couldn't do that with two kids. I was also unemployed and struggling with substance abuse issues.

Our lives were broken. Oh, and all four of us were homeless.

Those were the life stories Christine, Bill, Amy and I were given at the beginning of Richmond's annual "Walking in Their Shoes" event, organized by Homeward, a nonprofit working on behalf of the homeless. At the start of the day, at a center across the street from the city jail, we were given two bus tickets worth $1.50 each and the names of several Richmond agencies. After being instructed to take only $5 and one form of identification, we set out to find help.

Two things: First, don't just dismiss these situations as outlandish, drummed up for "Walking in Their Shoes." They have, in fact, been drawn from Homeward's files. And new files continue to be created.

Second, every major faith on the planet believes it's our responsibility to care for our poor and downtrodden. I learned that there's a small but determined army of utterly committed individuals and groups in Richmond doing this work, right now.

There is the case manager at Richmond's Department of Social Services who routinely goes looking for the homeless under bridges, in their encampments, and in alleys, offering them rescue from the streets. She is not a big, scary person. Not even close—yet she often goes alone.

She is the only person I've ever met who began a sentence, "I met this guy under a bridge on Chamberlayne…"

There is the social worker who runs a program for victims of domestic violence. She will see to it that frightened and injured women and children are whisked away from danger and into a safe location, any hour of the day or night. Her name is familiar to numerous Richmond hotel desk clerks because she rents so many rooms so regularly.

She is the only person I know who's ever dealt with a man who told his wife and children, "If you leave, I'll kill the dog."

"They'd probably already seen him kick the dog across the room," she said. "How could a mother and child find the strength to walk out then?"

There's the volunteer at a downtown church's lunch

program for the homeless who patiently helped oversee lunch for a crowd of a couple hundred.

She's the only person who's ever told me, "Lots of people look at people who are homeless and poor and say, 'They just ought to pull themselves up by their bootstraps.' Well, these folks don't have bootstraps."

There are others who are helping out. Plenty of others. They're not naïve; they know some people are out to milk the system, to sponge whatever they can. But the work, and the people they do it for, are too important. Plus, experience has offered valuable lessons: "We know the ones who are playing games," a human services assistant at city offices told me.

They also know there will be situations they just can't fix. But they go to work every day and stand up for people who often can't stand up for themselves. They'd have done all they could for us, too, if we'd been for real. And there's no shortage of real.

In our own way, many of us are trying to do God's work, but some of these folks seem to know and feel it more. And see it on more faces, more often.

(Shrugs Shoulders)

"I don't know" can be three of the most refreshing words in the English language. If you say them honestly, it means you don't feel compelled to impress anyone by seeming to know more than you really do, and that you're willing to admit there are things you don't have answers to.

This is hard for some people.

Here's an example of the phrase used humbly and well: Famed evangelist Billy Graham visited New Orleans in the wake of Hurricane Katrina and, during his tour of the resulting devastation, he was asked by a reporter what he would tell people who ask him how a loving God could let something like this happen. Here, in part, is what he said: "Well, I asked myself why, and I don't know why. There's no way I can know."

Maybe the stark honesty of Graham's response is one of the reasons he's so widely respected. Among believers of all stripes, there's no shortage of people who seem to know what God is thinking—and are quite willing to speak for Him. On the heels of many natural disasters and tragedies, someone almost always pipes up to pronounce why God "did this." There are some, even some religious leaders, who can tell you just how angry God is about a certain court case, election or event, and how He might choose to demonstrate the degree of His displeasure.

But when it comes to discerning God's thoughts and motivations, the truth often is, as far as I can see, that we just don't know. Part of what God seems to ask of us, and this can be excruciating, is to sometimes accept what comes our way without necessarily understanding why. Instead of knowing, we're sometimes asked to trust.

This is not to say that God operates at random. I don't think life's a crapshoot; nor is it, I believe, an intellectual cop-out to say that we can't fathom the Almighty. I think

God has made his basic goals pretty clear, but there is much that remains a mystery. And that is as it should be, because if we could explain God, He wouldn't be a "higher power"—and we wouldn't need Him. Deep down, we want a God who is beyond our ability to completely comprehend.

A few years ago, I went to the hospital room of a five-year-old girl and spent some time with her parents shortly before the doctors declared their little girl dead. She'd struggled with serious health problems since birth; all of her years had been difficult ones. I'm convinced that no one, religious leader or otherwise, can adequately explain how a loving God would allow such a difficult and painful situation to go on for five years and then end so sadly. But this girl's parents clung to their belief in a God who loves their daughter, and them, and her funeral was an amazing celebration of that faith. If you were to ask them why their family suffered so, they probably couldn't tell you, just as they probably couldn't give you a list of reasons for their faith during those difficult times.

For some things, there are just no answers in this lifetime. It takes a certain amount of humility to acknowledge that. That's one of the reasons that it can be so frustrating when people make pronouncements about what God is thinking or doing in a certain situation—there is little humility there.

With hurricanes, tsunamis and other natural disasters, does God have a strategy we can understand? Does He with political events, terrorism, or with the sickness or death of people we love, or with our personal struggles?

I don't know. And, because of that, trusting such a God is a challenge.

I do, however, believe this, taken from a prayer written by German pastor Dietrich Bonhoeffer as he languished in a Nazi prison during World War II: "Your ways are past understanding, but You know the way for me."

Hopping Down the Bunny Trail? Not So Much

I'm not really sure how this whole Easter Bunny thing came about, with all the hippity-hopping, egg-hiding and choco-late-distributing. And I realize he's built quite a following, but I'd like to nominate another animal to be Easter's mascot.

I'm thinking goat. A goat would be perfect.

In pre-Jesus Biblical times, during the annual obser-vance of a Jewish holy day called the Day of Atonement, which was meant to wipe away the sins of the people, cer-emonies included a symbolic tradition involving two goats. Both animals would be brought to the temple and present-ed to the high priest. Then, by drawing lots, one would be chosen "for the Lord" and the other became the scapegoat.

The goat "for the Lord" became part of the ritual sacri-fice offered by the high priest on behalf of the people.

The scapegoat's fate was very different. The high priest lay his hands on this goat to represent the sins of the people being placed on it. Then the goat was taken far, far away and released so deep into the wilderness that it had no chance of finding its way back.

The scapegoat demonstrated that the guilt of all was

removed and would never return. It reminded the people of the words of the Psalmist: "As far as the east is from the west, so far has he removed our transgressions from us."

Then Jesus came along, and that's why a goat is such a perfect Easter symbol. Because he went to the cross, taking on the sins of the people, and because He came out of the grave, Jesus is now the scapegoat to end all scapegoats. Our guilt is now as far removed from us as the east is from the west. It cannot, and will not, ever return.

As one well-known pastor put it, "The goat has left the building."

Truly, that goat will never be seen again. Happy Easter, indeed!

The Best Gifts are the
Unexpected Ones

When I was a single 20-something, I worked for a few years for a company that, instead of a cash Christmas bonus, shipped me a couple fancy-dancy wine glasses every year. The glasses had a little green sticker on them that said Waterford Crystal, which meant absolutely nothing to me.

I remember stashing the glasses in a kitchen cabinet in my apartment, grumbling about how a check would have been way cooler. By the time Cathy and I were engaged, I had stashed six of them.

Not long before the wedding, Cathy packed them up and went to a now-defunct Richmond department store, "returned" them—and walked out with our first-ever mattress and box spring in exchange. I was flabbergasted. The bed was quality stuff, and all we had to do to get it was clear out some glasses I thought were semi-worthless. I had only used one a time or two, and I'm almost positive I ran it through the dishwasher, which people tell me is a significant faux pas when dealing with crystal.

These days, I'm pretty sure that mattress and box spring are taking up space in a landfill somewhere, but I thought about them during this season of unexpected gifts.

There's something especially spirit-lifting about an unexpected gift. Almost all gifts are fun, but even more so, I think, are the ones you really didn't see coming.

Several years ago, before Facebook ruled the world, a good friend was celebrating a milestone birthday. Her husband hatched a plan, spread the word as widely as he could, and my friend ending up spending the day alternately laughing and crying as she read her way through a deluge of unanticipated birthday e-mails.

Another friend, knowing her time on earth was growing short, used some of it to leave a series of handwritten notes for her husband strategically concealed around their home. He found comfort and a deep gratitude in her effort and in her knowledge of what he'd need to know when she was gone. He also learned to do the laundry.

Christmas comes bearing an interesting combination of both a sense of expectation and a sense of not knowing exactly what to expect.

Mary, a young Jewish woman living in the Middle East a couple thousand years ago, certainly didn't expect the appearance of an angel or the news he brought with him: You're pregnant, despite the fact that you and your fiancé, Joseph, haven't done what it normally takes to get that way. The baby will not only be a miracle, but God's own son. At enormous personal risk, Mary said, "May it be to me as you have said."

What an unexpected gift that turned out to be.

Joseph didn't expect the news his fiancée brought him, either: We—yes, we—are going to have a son. Technically, you're not his father, but you're a big part of this miracle, too. There were several ways Joseph could have chosen to make this little bit of potential scandal go away, and must have been sorely tempted to do so. The option he picked was to marry Mary and raise the child as his own.

What an unexpected gift that turned out to be.

No one really expected that when that child was born, in a grubby manger that was home to a few farm animals in an obscure village, it would change everything. Literally everything. Today, most of the world dates its calendar from the day of that birth. In less than a week, most of the world will pause to remember and celebrate the arrival of that boy, whose parents named him Jesus, as the angel had instructed.

He has turned out, for more people than we could ever count, to be the most important unexpected gift of all. Merry Christmas, indeed.

About the Author

Tom Allen has been a writer and journalist for 30 years and a regular contributor to the Faith & Values column of the *Richmond Times-Dispatch* for the last five. He has served as the editor of the *Virginia Journal of Education* since 1990. His columns have appeared in newspapers and magazines across Virginia and in the *Pittsburgh Post-Gazette*.

He lives in Richmond, Virginia with Cathy, his wife of nearly 30 years. They have three grown children, Andy, Amy and Emily, of whom they're ridiculously proud.

You can contact Tom at GraceHappensBook@gmail.com.

www.ingramcontent.com/pod-product-compliance
Lightning Source LLC
Jackson TN
JSHW011411130125
77033JS00024B/968